DATE DUE

OCT 1 3 2018	

The Social Media Manifesto

THE SOCIAL MEDIA MANIFESTO

Jed Hallam

palgrave
macmillan

First published 2013 by
PALGRAVE MACMILLAN

Palgrave Macmillan in the UK is an imprint of Macmillan Publishers Limited, registered in England, company number 785998, of Houndmills, Basingstoke, Hampshire RG21 6XS.

Palgrave Macmillan in the US is a division of St Martin's Press LLC, 175 Fifth Avenue, New York, NY 10010.

Palgrave Macmillan is the global academic imprint of the above companies and has companies and representatives throughout the world.

Palgrave® and Macmillan® are registered trademarks in the United States, the United Kingdom, Europe and other countries.

ISBN 978–1–137–27141–9

This book is printed on paper suitable for recycling and made from fully managed and sustained forest sources. Logging, pulping and manufacturing processes are expected to conform to the environmental regulations of the country of origin.

A catalogue record for this book is available from the British Library.

A catalog record for this book is available from the Library of Congress.

10 9 8 7 6 5 4 3 2 1
22 21 20 19 18 17 16 15 14 13

Printed and bound in Great Britain by
CPI Antony Rowe, Chippenham and Eastbourne

Acknowledgments

I would like to sincerely thank the following people for their help, contribution, advice and support over the last 18 months in the research and writing of this book. Without your support, this book would not have been possible.

My friends and mentors Dominic Stinton and Graham Drew, two of the smartest people I have ever met. Everyone at VCCP Share for listening to my seemingly endless out-loud thinking and for being incredibly supportive during the whole process—Annabell, Rob, Tom and Dave, Claire, Lulu, Billy, Sophie and Nincs have all shown tireless enthusiasm for my seemingly illogical train of thought and have helpfully put my brain back on track when it has veered off course.

The whole of the VCCP Partnership, but specifically Stephanie Brimacombe, Rob Wills, Fred Rodwell and Andy Parsons, Cydney, Rob Dougan, Boothy, Tim Kitell, Fergus, Barney, Tracey, Charles Vallance, Adrian Colman, David Boscawen, Jon Phillips and last, but most certainly not least, Dando and Dodd.

Ged Carroll, Mat Morisson, Becky McMichael, Tim Hoang, Tim Malbon, Stephen Waddington, Nathan Williams, Antony Mayfield, James Whatley, Michael Cooper, my old family at Wolfstar Consultancy (but specifically Tim Sinclair and Stuart Bruce), Gabbi Cahane, Philip Sheldrake and all the guys at Meanwhile.

Contents

Contents

List of Figures

Foreword

This is a book about change. Indeed, in many ways, it's a manual on change; a "how to" guide to social media and its impact on business and business communication.

If Jed had wanted to, and his publisher had allowed him, he could have expanded the scope to include politics, arts, social activisim and, even, sex and religion. This thing called social media, like the internet on which it rides, has quite an appetite. There are few parts of life it leaves un-nibbled.

It is, however, to Jed's credit that he stuck to a tighter brief. Wherever possible he has avoided generalisations and extrapolations. Instead he offers examples and practical advice to anyone who is wrestling with how they adapt their organisation to a newly socialialised reality. Moreover, in the tradition of the great "how to" books of yesteryear, Jed has clearly given plenty of thought to how his readers will use the book, which bits will be of most interest depending on their requirements and, therefore, how it can be most easily and fruitfully navigated.

On top of all these splendid qualities, this is also a book that, like a fat kid taking up weightlifting, starts with a big natural advantage in that it concerns an inherently interesting subject.

When I started in advertising back in the 80's, one of my first bosses, a pipe-smoking Yorkshireman, would often mutter disapprovingly about the tendency for everyone to approach advertising with an open mouth. Those days are gone. No-one talks about advertising any more, it's merely "a tax you pay for being boring". Now it's social media that gets everyone yacking. More pertinently, it doesn't just get them yacking. It IS them yacking. And that's why it's gold dust. For the first time ever we can measure it. We can monitor it. We can interact with it. We can even shape it. And we can do all these things better once we've read this book. Indeed, I would go so far as to issue a guarantee that you will change at least 5 of the ways your business communicates as a result of reading this book, or the publisher will give you your money back.

Another advantage of social media is that it arouses strong opinions. Some love it, some hate it. It has its champions and its detractors, its victims and culprits. And whilst sometimes, despite all the billionaires it has created, old fogies like me can be tempted to think its importance, in time, may slacken—that the pendulum may swing back, not to where it used to be, but where the frantic over-sharing of everything (imho) begins to wane—despite all this, what emerges from Jed's book are three incontrovertible trends;

- The way customers communicate about and with brands/companies/institutions is changing beyond recognition
- Therefore the way companies/brands/institutions communicate with customers must change by a similar order of magnitude
- Therefore the way companies/brands/institutions communicate internally needs to change fundamentally

I could write at length on each of these three subjects but the good news is that Jed already has. So I won't. Not least because I would give a rather amateurish perspective, whereas Jed provides expert analysis and practical guidance on what these changes entail and their implications (not least the importance of Gephi, and open source graph visualisation platforms in general) in terms of what you need to do next.

However, where I think a little reflection is in order is to do with a wider point regarding the nature of change, because sometimes its symptoms can get muddled up with its causes—and nowhere more so than in the world of social media. One of the peculiar qualities of social, converged technology is the massive contradictions inherent within it. Commentatotors, including Jed, are quick to point out how it spells the end of business as we know it, that the rule of tyrannical brands is over. But the problem with this assertion is that it goes hand in hand with a dramatic rise in exactly what is supposed to be disappearing, namely vast, all conquering global brands that exercise something close to a monopolistic hold on their categories. Anything much over 35% market share tended to be viewed as anti competitive before the advent of the internet, nowadays it is not uncommon in online markets to see brands with well over 75% market share. Despite the internet's ability to create unprecedentedly favourable conditions for small, niche, specialist brands (the famous long tail), it also creates perfect conditions for "default settings" where it simply becomes more convenient for everyone, apart from the most initiated, to adopt the dominant protocol, often on the illusory basis that it's free.

It is true, then, that the internet is great for small brands, social enterprise and collaborative consumption. What is less often stressed is that it is also great for the corporate colossi, where power seems to be increasingly concentrated into a smallish number of global super brands which operate both on and offline. Whether this fully represents progress is to be debated.

Similarly, the internet is widely associated with greater fluidity, a breaking down of hierarchical structures and loss of control. Yet many of the greatest exponents of the online world are immensely controlling, trying to coral users into a single operating system, continually requiring the customer to submit to various terms and conditions (which, to be honest, none of us but Jed understand) and, it has to be said, exerting remarkably tight control over the levels of tax they pay to foreign governments and customers. There are some marvellous exceptions to the new control freaks, there are some fantastic open platforms, and some visionary business leaders who are determined to create a truly open system. But, ironically, these often come from more traditional industries, with more traditional and transparent business models.

Another aspect of the new era of control is Big Data. The rise of the CDO, the CIO and the CTO does not entirely sit happily with the idea of a more fluid, unregimented business style. In fact in many ways it feels Orwellian. This is another of the great contradictions of the internet, whilst at one level we are much freer, we are in other ways ever more trapped and more surveilled.

A similar point could be made about the nature of sharing over social networks. This is something that has been brilliantly covered by Sherry Turkle in her thought provoking book Alone Together, so I will simply paraphrase her argument, which is that the type of sharing that we associate with social networks isn't really sharing at all, in that it creates the illusion of companionship when in fact much of the world is becoming a lonelier place. Thus the rise of the micro network, which is likely to offer more depth and meaning than the scattergun social graph. But then micro networks aren't hugely different from coffee mornings, and they've been around for ages.

Which brings me to my final point about technological change. The most successful technologies tend to help us be more like we already are, they tend to go with the grain of human behaviour, because human behaviour is close to constant and not even the mightiest online brands can change that. This means that where we see technology adopted it tends, ironically, to leave things as they were, only more so. We can be a judgemental and resentful species, social media allows us to air more of our resentments and squabbles (ask any Premiership footballer). We can also be altruistic and consensual, which is why we are seeing the rise of collaborative consumption, micro finance and task sharing.

Organisationally, the impact of a converged, internetegrated (™) world cannot be underestimated, and Jed's book is a brilliant manual on how to respond. But have things truly changed? To say that we are more beholden to our customers, our staff, our stakeholders is irrefutable. But are we any more so than when George Cadbury built Bournville as a model town for his employees? It is conceivable that what we are witnessing is surface change, and that the fundamentals of business, society and branding remain permanent. If you want to succeed in the long run, be good to your customer, be good to your staff, and be good to your community. There are plenty of corporate goliaths who forgot this recently and, like Oxymandias, king of kings, are now face down in the dirt.

If there is one thing I take from Jed's book, it is a re-affirmation of classic marketing principles; listen to your customer, learn and adapt accordingly, communicate this to your staff and then begin the process all over the again. Only this time with bells on. As Tancredi Falconeri says to his uncle Don Fabrizio Corbera, Prince of Salina in Prince Giuseppe Tomasi di Lampedusa's posthumous and melancholy masterpiece Il Gattopardo (The Leopard); "Everything must change so that everything can stay the same". Try tweeting that.

Charles Vallance
Founder of the VCCP Partnership

Introduction

The premise of this book is simple: it should provide a brief introduction into the changes that have taken place in business over the previous 15 years, it should outline why "social media" is not about technology but human insight, and finally, it should clearly illustrate how you can use this insight to develop an innovative and competitive business. The way in which I have pieced this book together makes it part short essays and part pragmatic guide to using this changing landscape as an opportunity to turn your business into a social business.

You will be presented with a detailed breakdown of how human insight can be used across your business and an insight (I believe) into the next ten years backed up by some of the finest economic, technological and strategic thinkers of the last one hundred years (obviously not me). Also, where possible, I have referenced best-practice case studies to help illustrate the potential that becoming a social business represents.

While some of the points I make may seem academic, please bear with me, I will get to the actionable stuff in good time, but first it is important to give a macro view of what has happened to create (as my friend and mentor Stephen Waddington coined as the title of his excellent book) *Brand Anarchy*.

This book is about how and why business has changed, and how you can use this change to build a stronger, more profitable business.

***

My research for this book began a few years ago. I was in Paris for a week ahead of moving to London, I left with no plans and a stack of books—one of those books was Nassim Taleb's *The Black Swan*. I bought it on the recommendation of a friend, but thought it bore little relation to my day to day work, as it was about fragility and economic instability in the financial markets. In the space of two days I read the book cover to cover, and what struck me most pertinently was how the unpredictable behavior Taleb was describing in action in the financial markets was also being replicated in a more micro-level in different markets—namely, how many businesses were struggling to understand how the influx of consumer data from social media and the increase in availability of communications would affect their business. The level of complexity of business had increased, as had access to technology. Taleb talks a lot about the mistakes that many traders make in being too close to the markets, news and information and how micro-analysis of data caused massive issues on a macro-scale. In short, the financial markets had always been complex, but traders had become more simplistic in their approach, due to technology—the parallels with branding and business building were uncanny. The industrial revolution gave way to mass production of products, the division of labor coined by Adam Smith (and later developed by Karl Marx) ensured that businesses could produce huge quantities of the same product—which had a knock on effect in the late 1950s and 1960s when the rise of advertising and "branding" lead many of these businesses to use advertising and branding as a way to create salience in stagnant, identikit markets—hundreds of identical products lined the supermarket shelves, distinguished from each other not by the products themselves, but from the branding wrapped around them by advertising agencies. Technology had made mass production easy, and businesses lazy. Consumers obviously discussed products and services, giving advice to their friends and family, but this was kept within small networks of people—location ensured word of mouth had a limited impact, and it was easy for brands to mass-broadcast messaging into millions of homes through television and radio advertising. As the Internet began to gain critical mass, 40 years later, and access became cheaper, we saw a proliferation of online journals and IRC (early versions of chat rooms and forums), platforms for people to discuss any subject without boundaries. This gave the everyday consumer a voice that could be potentially heard by anyone with a modem, breaking those geographical word of mouth boundaries that had existed for thousands of years. Then, as Gordon E. Moore predicted, technology became cheaper, more prolific, and today more people have mobile telephone access than have access to clean water. This has flattened any notion of geographical boundaries, aided by platforms such as blogs, Facebook, YouTube and Twitter. Everyone with access to the Internet can have a voice, and if their voice is compelling or interesting enough, people will listen. Just ask Justin Bieber, whose career was launched from a YouTube page.

This increase in consumer power (let us call it that for argument's sake) through technology has increased the levels of complexity wrapped around businesses, and this complexity makes stability and prediction virtually impossible. Prior to Taleb's work in *The Black Swan,* Louis Bachelier, the founding father of financial mathematics, wrote about the role of complexity in relation to markets in the opening to his 1900 thesis, *Theorie de la Speculation*:

> The factors that determine activity on the Exchange are innumerable, with events, current or expected, often bearing no apparent relation to price variation. Beside the somewhat natural causes for variation come artificial causes: the Exchange reacts to itself, and the current trading is a function, not only of prior trading, but also of it is relationship to the rest of the market.

The point that Bachelier made (and was subsequently snubbed by academia and economists for—at least initially) is that the stock market is a complex organism that develops from multiple sources that are almost certainly not predictable. In the past century we have seen numerous market crashes, and yet very few people have been able to predict them. Yet for the last century we have tried to minimize this complexity with mathematical models, boiling down incredibly complex events into processable inputs to be fed into the financial "black box" as Benoit Mandelbrot calls it, so that we can predict the outcome.

The same "reductionism" is at play in business too, and we have degenerated in our understanding of business, from the early days of mercantilism (in which businesses and merchants were forced to understand the buyer, less they not eat that night) we have increasingly tried to force human (or market, even) behaviors into systems, models, processes and technology. In trying to better "scale" our businesses, we have looked for shortcuts to make more money, at the expense of people (and usually, what follows, our businesses).

So why, if on a macro-financial level we have invested a century of thinking from Nobel prize-winning economists, mathematicians and physicists, were we not able to predict the crash of 2008? Or the dot-com bubble? Because people are unpredictable, and therefore the markets and businesses that they operate within become unpredictable.

For thousands of years philosophers have studied the human condition, trying to capture our motivations, our morals, predicting and theorizing around our behavior. Taking the complex system (our brain) and trying to explain it within simple words so that our brains can understand it. A great artist can capture this human condition in a painting, a poem or a thought. A musician can generate a similar effect with music or a lyric. Yet economists, scientists and businesses (outside of a few outliers) repeatedly fail to understand the human condition. Since the advent of the "business consultant" (the anonymous Norwegian who wrote *The Kings Mirror* in 1250), we have collectively spent millennia trying to understand the "human truth" to help businesses better craft messaging around a product to sell more of that product—ignoring the fact that that the moment we actually capture that "human truth," it is just as likely to have evaporated. Humans are complex animals, with unpredictable behaviors, and empirical evidence helps us to only prove what has happened before, rather than what is yet to come. In one of his many aphorisms in *The Bed of Procrustes,* Nassim Nicholas Taleb states:

> What made medicine fool people for so long was that its successes were predominately displayed and its mistakes (literally) buried.[1]

How many businesses have you seen spend years crafting a product around a need or human truth from a specific point in time, only to launch it months (or years) later and fail? It is widely suggested that nine out of ten start-up businesses fail, yet we continue to use sterile, clinical methods, models and research to create products for people. People are complex, fickle and unpredictable.

What has slightly altered the game on human unpredictability, however, is technology. The effect that this has is very simple—with greater access to technology and the Internet comes wider networks of communication. The best way of explaining this effect is by using some simple network terminology—a network is a collection of people with shared connections (imagine listing out all of your friends and then drawing lines between each for how they know (or do not know) each other). A network with a high density of connections between friends is a strong network, and usually this can be assumed to be based on either location or a shared interest. Now imagine a much wider network that features many different characteristics and many "weak ties" into other, new, networks (for example I have one friend who is an Olympic skier)—these new networks are classed as your "weak ties," your way into new friendship circles and your point of exposure to new information. What the Internet has done is create a giant "weak tie" network where it is now possible to stay connected and make connections to almost anyone in the world—thus exposing your exposure to new information too. The effect that this has on businesses is that customers that may have once been unable to connect with one another can now easily find each other and discuss your company—for the better or worse. (One key thing to note is that "word of mouth," "viral" and negativity around brands is not new—it is just that the ability to share this information with the wider world is new.)

This new level of connectivity allows for symmetrical dialogue between brands and its consumers (and employees, but we will come on to that later)—providing a huge volume of new data, or Big Data as it is now commonly referred to as. Pulling this back to Bachelier, if we can identify more sources of data (or inputs into Mandelbrot's *Black Box*) then we can begin to build a bigger picture of unpredictability, helping us to define the known unknowns, and in turn, the unknown unknowns. Umberto Eco stocked his library with endless books he never read so that he could narrow down the unknown unknowns; if we can do the same with Big Data then we can at least begin to challenge human unpredictability, rather than throwing more mathematical models at it. There are two fundamental changes to the business landscape, and they are both inextricably tied to each other; technology and complexity. Throughout the next 14 chapters, I will hopefully explain how you can use both technology and complexity to improve your business, rather than let both of them erode your profits. There is a single-minded message to this book, and that is that humans are complex, not because of technology but because of our nature—if, as businesses, we can begin to understand the complexity that this produces, and react to it appropriately, our businesses can be stronger.

This is not a book for the modern MBA student, or a tick list of things to do with technology, or even a handbook for building a social business, in many ways. This book aims to highlight that if we understand humans better, we can build better businesses that provide products that people want to buy, that make people's lives better, and that (ultimately) help to build sustainable, conscientious and profitable businesses. The use of technology is merely a means to understand humans and markets more comprehensively.

CHAPTER 1

The Death of "Brand"

Michael Wolff and Wally Olins pioneered the concept of brand-ing, setting up Wolff Olins in Camden in the 1960s and since then they have continued to push the boundaries beyond packaging and design and into new spaces—including digital spaces. In 2011 Wolff worked with Intel to produce a piece of content for Intel's Visual Life project. The video is filled with great sound bites from Wolff, who talks mainly about design, aesthetics and the concept of brand, but one of the standout comments from the video is:

> A brand is really a way of remembering what something is like, for future reference. Something you value, something you feel attracted to.

On the surface, this comment is purely about the aesthetics of a brand, but I think Wolff is being much broader than design. In a world of increasingly visual communications (not from a design point of view but from the point of view of being able to actually *see* communications) it is important to realize the impact that this has on the brand—we can see the logo, the marketing materials, the advertising, but now we also see the conversations going on around a brand. This has an interesting effect, if we are to believe Krugman's theory of Effective Frequency (in which he believes that there is a certain number of times someone has to see some-thing before they remember it), which would now have many more inputs than before the digital evolution. Conversation is part of the fabric of the brand, and we can see it everywhere.

So the big question resting over the future of brand perception is who is responsible for it? In the old world of one way communica-tions it used to be the public relations and advertising department (both of which would produce the only "visible" brand commu-nications on behalf of the business), but in a world where your potential and existing customers are talking more frequently and having greater access to people across your whole organization, that is simply not the case any more—which begs the question, "how do we control our brand perception?" Well, the best way to shape your brand perception has not changed, your brand has to listen to its customers, react to them and learn from them, but now it is in real time, making it a job for the whole business. From the customer service department through to the IT team, everyone represents your business now because communications has been flattened out. If there is someone in your market research team who has been treated badly by the CEO, a few tweets or blog posts later the whole world may potentially know the situation. In modern brand building, the whole business is responsible, and this requires the business leaders to have a fundamental understanding of why and how. We can no longer rely on packaging and design to create salience in the supermarket aisles, when people potentially have a constant stream of information being delivered to them about your business.

Douglas Rushkoff, arguably one of the most influential commentators on digital culture believes that "the web is biased towards non-fiction"—people are looking for facts and information on products, especially during a time of economic uncertainty when each purchase has to deliver on its promise.

Take, for instance, the insurance industry in the UK where consumer loyalty dropped to 20 percent in 2011.[1] If you take this drop in loyalty, and map it against the volume of people using Google to search for advice and reviews around insurance products (around 12 million monthly searches[2]), you can see that people are looking for facts and information. If we then take this data and add in information in the fall of trust of brands from the 2012 Edelman Trust Barometer, you can see that searching for reviews and advice online has become a huge part of consumer behavior; in fact, 60 percent of consumer journeys[3] that end in purchase online, start with search. So this heady combination of changing consumer behavior, deference to brand voice and preference to consumer reviews makes search engines a large part of your business's brand image. What makes this even more interesting is the way in which search engines like Google prioritize "social" search results—giving forums like MoneySavingExpert and MoneySupermarket a huge level of influence (they have a combined monthly reach of more than 20million users)—especially when you consider that in the insurance industry, more than 30 percent of all conversations taking place in these two forums are direct complaints about brands. Your brand is being represented not by the advertising or messaging that you promote, but by the product or service reviews that people find when they search for your brand.

This obviously puts a huge emphasis on the product, not the brand. That is not to say that people do not still care about brands and storytelling, but unless your story is backed up by a great product, people are not going to buy into both. In a world of absolute consumer truth, your search engine results are king.

One of the major issues with this is that there is a tendency toward negativity in digital spaces—a negative experience is much more easily shared (due to the anonymous nature of much of the digital space) than a positive experience. This is a basic human truth (especially in the UK, where moaning is a competitive sport)—basic analysis of the major personal finance forums reveals that almost 95 percent of conversations taking place are either neutral (mostly statement based) or negative (with 30% directed specifically at brands). This makes for a challenging space for brand reputation— the brand has to respond to customer issues for two specific reasons: (1) to resolve a customer issue, and (2) to be visibly resolving customer issues (remember the 1:9:90 cliche, 1% of people create content, 9% of people comment on it, yet 90% of people see that content—so each customer complaint is seen by potentially 10,000,000 people)—leaving complaints unresolved is akin to refusing to answer customer complaints in the call center. With this in mind, huge above-the-line campaign amplification campaigns merely paper over the cracks created by substandard products or services. A great example of this is when Orange, the telecommunications brand, decided to launch a Twitter account for Orange Wednesdays (its flagship entertainment campaign)—very quickly the Twitter feed was filled with customer service complaints— purely because Orange decided to launch a brand campaign rather than deal with very direct business issues.

James Dyson, the creator of arguably one of the most successful brands of our times gave a talk at a Wired conference in early 2012 called Disruption by Design at which he stated that the only word that is banned at Dyson is the word "brand"; "we are only as good as our latest product. I do not believe in brand at all." Now this obviously generated a huge amount of discussion, most of which pointed at the fact that Dyson spends a huge amount of money on advertising every year, but the product is what people care about and Dyson has a rich heritage of always focusing on the product benefits, rather than the brand story, much like Apple.

With such an increasing focus on product benefits, what role is brand supposed to play? Well, with brands such as Nike and Coca Cola, the story becomes an integral part.

There is a fantastic parable in Sun Tzu's *The Art of War* that describes the role of the king and the villagers. Tzu says that the king who builds himself a castle and never walks among the villagers will always provoke revolt, yet the king who lives with the villagers and walks among them every day will always be a man of the people. We have lived for too long under tyrannical brands that have dictated our tastes and our buyer behavior—and, as with politics over the last century, technology is giving power back to people. Brands that listen to their consumers and employees, that are not just seen to care, but actually care, are finding themselves in strong positions. Those that play ignorant to their audience are starting to crumble, with few exceptions (although of course there are exceptions). Businesses that are tightly guarded by "brand guardians" and public relations agencies provoke intrigue, inspection and (mostly) invite critical examination—in fact the lack of trust that consumers have in these "brand guardians" has continuously fallen since the late 1990s. Yet those brands that practice "open" and transparent behavior find themselves in a much stronger position—people understand that they listen, people are not fed the press release, they have conversations with real people from within the company.

Take a minute to think about which employees, in your business, come into contact with the general public everyday. It is everyone. Unless you are running a business from the outer reaches of the Arctic Circle, without an Internet connection and employing only reclusive people, your employees are going to have their own social networks and through social media they have access (and people have access to them) far beyond the four walls of your business. Information about your business will be spreading through those networks as we speak. Networks are absolutely integral to understanding and measuring perceptions of your brand.

Let us take an example, in Figure 1, the black dots are employees, the gray lines are relationships and the gray dots are non-employees.

Business X has 30 employees, and each is professionally connected to each other like the figure below:

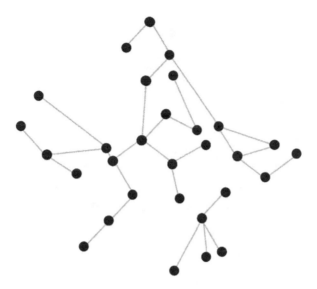

Figure 1　Traditional hierarchical business network

Now, let us look at how they socialize with each other in and out of work (see Figure 2):

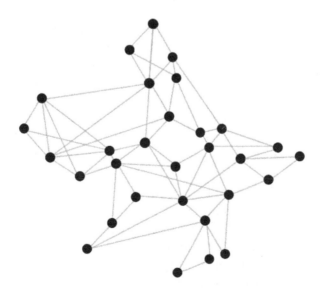

Figure 2　Actual social network within the organisation

Now, let us look at their immediate social networks outside of your business (see Figure 3):

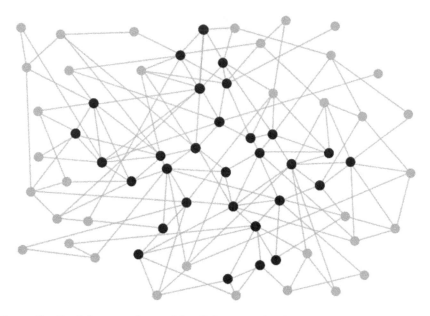

Figure 3   Social network outside of the organisation

It is easy to see how quickly a message could spread from inside the business (regardless of the department) to a much wider network (see Figure 4)—which, when you consider that the socio-logical theory of six degrees of separation was recently reduced to 4.2, indicates that within a matter of hours that message could have traveled the globe. (The originators of the message are high-lighted in light grey; the recipients of the message are highlighted in black.)

What is evident from this basic analysis is that what people know about your brand is not as simple as running an advertising cam-paign or securing editorial coverage in a national newspaper. Your people are your brand, and the conversations that they have with their wider networks are how brand perceptions are built. If you can understand how your employees are connected to one another and understand their social graphs (networks), you can begin to understand your brand perception.

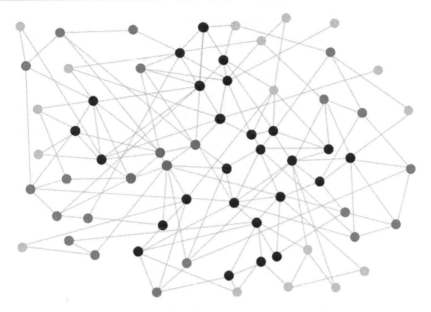

Figure 4   Flow of information within that social network

THE SINGLE BRAND

As you have seen, the concept of the single brand is difficult to attain. What used to be the domain of the public relations or advertising department now rests across the whole business and this makes singularity of the brand message complicated. However, the problem that technology and networks causes is also the solution. If you can begin to understand how your workforce are connected (outside of traditional hierarchical structures), then you can begin to understand how your brand message (or any message) is spread. While this sounds daunting, it is in fact relatively simple—analyze email logs. Speaking with the IT department and analyzing the email logs is basic statistical analysis, if you then take this data and run it through a simple graphing program such as Gephi then you can begin to match the social network of your organization against the formal structure of your business. This may seem like a very basic move, but very few brands have done this, one key example is the way in which IBM structures its core teams. IBM has a detailed database of employee information, explaining strengths, weaknesses and social connections—allowing it to construct highly functioning teams that appease all client needs while functioning like a well-oiled machine (due to their social structure, rather than their hierarchical structure). This type of approach breaks both hierarchical boundaries, while playing up to the most positive of group dynamics. This is the type of freeform team construction that is necessary for controlling (or at least monitoring) brand perception.

Perception control in an age of ubiquitous technological access is difficult (I used to work with a major mobile handset manufacturer whose analysts used to respond to consumer questions on forums without permission from their line manager, the correct information or tracking of the conversation—making leaks very difficult to track), however, there are a few simple principles you can adhere to in order to move toward a concentrated brand idea;

- Create a central place for all brand information to be stored (available to everyone, without discrimination).
- Create a set of guidelines for conversations that take place outside of the workplace (frequently called social media guidelines, but more importantly seen as communications guidelines).
- Analyze the social networks of each employee, in an effort to understand their personal networks (people attract friends like themselves, so a technician involved in research and development is likely to have similar friends (at competing brands))—this can be done through either Facebook, Twitter or through in-bound link analysis on their blog (however, arguably, Facebook will prove more reliable as the majority of people on the network have higher barriers to "friend" status than on networks such as Twitter or a personal blog).
- Communicate regularly—this is often overlooked. Brand vision can (and should) change regularly, but it is important to communicate and discuss this just as frequently. As the founder, or managing director, you are expected to lead the business; however, feedback from employees (at the coal face of consumers) is invaluable. Ensure that there is a feedback loop (be that a suggestion box (or email) or an internal social network—there is a wonderful case study of American Express creating an internal social network in order to crowd-source ideas to reduce overheads—the best suggestion came from the janitor who suggested using timers on the office lighting—and saved the business millions of pounds in overhead per year. Ideas come from everywhere).

■ Be more human. Probably the biggest cultural change is destroying the hierarchical temperament of many businesses—if you buy into Steven Johnson's theory of the *adjacent possible* (and you should, it is biologically proven), then creativity (be it business or brand ideas) can come from any background or expertise. Having a very broad experience of business (and life in general) ensures that creativity flows—and creativity is the foundation of innovation. Listen to everyone, give everyone a voice.

The main focus of this chapter is to reiterate that the concept of "brand control" through the public relations or advertising function is dead. With technology putting the focus onto products, the next chapter will address how businesses have started to deal with the change, and how they can move forward to make an even bigger impact by embracing offline and online convergence.

CHAPTER 2

Embracing Convergence

Technology has broken down the invisible constructs that we have spent centuries building—the "walls" of our business no longer exist, and the people within the business, our employees, are also our consumers, and other businesses consumers, and they are talking to each other. Right now. Sharing information, insights and opinions through social platforms. The "network" is the population.

My (admittedly, slightly butchered) definition of convergence is based on Henry Jenkins' concept of media convergence, but with more focus on the individual. My definition is as follows:

> Convergence: the seamless experience of seeing no boundaries between our online and offline lives—total integration.

(My definition (like many other borrowed terms throughout this book) may be loosely connected, but for the purpose of ease reading this book, I would rather we agree on terms early on.)

There are two main factors that have come into play for businesses in the last ten years; technology and an increased exposure to the complexity of people. These two factors are by no means mutually exclusive—cheaper access to faster technology has empowered people and widened their personal reach in terms of communication and knowledge—but this means that we can now see much more of the rawness of people, the swings in their opinions and the totality of their experiences. People are becoming increasingly comfortable with technology in their lives—from becoming reliant on Google Maps, to streaming their favorite television programs directly into their lounge through NetFlix—technology has become completely ubiquitous and most of the time we do not know that we are even using it. This is closing (and in many cases, has closed) the gap that previously existed between our offline and online lives—the two have converged. Yet business has been slow to adapt to this change in consumer behavior—we are still writing our "digital" strategy and trying to shoe horn offline ideas into the online world, without realizing that they are one and the same, and then the same businesses desperately wonder why their training video has not "gone viral," or why their Twitter account that publishes jokes all day only has 15 followers—because this world is so new to many senior business leaders, but so often oversold by media commentators and agencies, it can be immediately disappointing unless your business is working with people that have experience in this space.

At the same time, as people become much more comfortable with technology and the two worlds collide, people are sharing more than ever. This has been massively accelerated through mobile technology—we are constantly connected and within seconds we can have shared what we are doing with (potentially) millions of people (there is even a psychological issue that is developing among people who spent a lot of time with their mobile phones, where when they have to switch them off, or they lose signal, they get withdrawal symptoms—with many psychologists suggesting that the strength of the withdrawal is similar to that of nicotine!).

The best example of this naturally networked sharing in action is probably Instagram. Instagram, for those that are unfamiliar, is a photo editing and sharing social platform that is built solely for mobile phones. It allows you to take a photo, edit it using filters, and then share it to various social networks. So, if you ran a high-end cocktail bar in Dubai, it is quite feasible that one of your customers would take a photo of a particularly exotic cocktail to share with their friends when they returned home from their trip, except online and offline convergence takes it a few steps further. The customer takes the photo, adds a filter, uploads it to Instagram (the first network of people to see the photo), they then choose to share their location to FourSquare (another network of people then sees their location and the photo), they also choose to share the photo to Facebook (which geo-tags the photo, which is seen by a third network of people) and Twitter (a fourth network of people!). Very quickly an offline experience that's taking place (potentially) thousands of miles away from the customers' friends has been seen by four different networks of people through social media. Then, if the customer chooses so, they can use one of the various Instagram printing services, and the photo can be turned into a mouse mat or fridge magnet (there is a whole cottage industry popping up around these types of service). This is offline–online convergence at its best—true integration between what used to be two different worlds, in order to enhance your experience and share your life with your friends.

Instagram is a fine consumer example, but let's take this one step further and a little closer to home; how about employees? Most people that work in an office will have a phone that can receive emails, which from the business point of view is great—the BlackBerry single-handedly signaled the end of the 9–5 job, giving the business direct access to its employees at any time of day and over the weekend. However, the same advances in technology also gave rise to social platforms such as Twitter and forums, places where your employees can talk with each other, people outside of your organization (potential customers) and (Gasp! Shock! Horror!) people that work at competitors'. So the same technology that has given you access to your employees, has also given them access to the rest of the world—and they are talking.

Not all of these conversations are the same though, and I believe that the Internet divides these conversations into two neat types of network graphs.

THE SOCIAL GRAPH

This is the network graph that depicts relationships between people based on (usually pre-existing) friendships—from school, work or industry conferences. People that, mostly, we have met in real life and consider to be friends.

THE INTEREST GRAPH

The interest graph is based on shared interests—so it's the communities that were part of both online and offline where we come together because we have a common interest thread. Think about book clubs, or parenting forums online. It's regular for people to move between the interest graph and into the social graph, as we become closer friends. However, from an employee point of view, the interest graph is going to be of most immediate interest to your business, as this is where employees are most likely to be discussing work in a sensitive manner.

The information that's being shared about your organization online and offline is having a direct impact on the perceptions that your employees have about your business. Information that used to be held behind internal walled gardens is now (mostly) freely available online—disgruntled ex-employees, pseudonymous blogs and existing employees with little discretion are helping to shape the impressions of your employees—and this lack of control scares businesses. The best way to combat this loss of control, however, is to *involve* your employees in the fabric of your business—share information with them, address issues that have been expressed online, and understand that they could (if they had the motivation) find virtually anything out about the business and share that internally and externally.

(I will be exploring internal communications in more depth in the Chapter 11.)

Convergence is difficult to adapt to because (usually) the leadership function was born into a world where online and offline *were* divided, so the concept of someone living their live in a truly integrated way seems alien.

However, there is a much bigger problem at play than technologically cultural differences between those in a leadership capacity of businesses and the so-called Generation Y, and the blame for this problem is planted firmly at the door of certain marketing agencies.

The changes in the business and branding landscape over the last ten years have seen lots of new forms of agency spring up. Agencies that sell "mobile solutions," SEO agencies, digital agencies, social media agencies, media companies that only buy Facebook advertising, agencies whose sole purpose is to run Twitter accounts—the list is endless. One of the challenges that all of these types of new agency have in common is that the type of work that they are doing should be much bigger than a simple addition to a marketing strategy, yet they are frequently selling "add-ons" and "quick-fixes" because they lack the education, experience or authority to explain how this new form of communications fits in to the clients business at a more strategic level, so the agency sells something smaller, and less costly, to get the initial business with the idea being that the agency can then "grow" to become more integrated and move further up the business hierarchy—however, in my experience in this industry, this very rarely happens, and this has a number of effects:

- Clients become used to "adding digital" on to campaigns.
- Agencies find it increasingly easy to sell, because clients find it easy to buy.

- Agencies then try and "productize" these add-ons and scale them across all clients.
- Clients struggle to measure or prove the ROI because the add-on is not tied to core business metrics.
- Agencies then struggle to find a more strategic positioning because they have been unable to prove the ROI on previous projects.

It is a vicious circle.

Worse than this is that because "digital" is still growing as a market, the barriers to entry (both for agencies and staff) are incredibly low—meaning that much of the "strategic advice" a brand receives is coming from someone without any wider marketing or business experience. In a book that I co-authored in 2011, *The Social Media MBA*, I explored the idea that the "digital" market was due to undergo a process that Hugo Hopenhayn called "The Shakeout." This is the process that most emerging markets go through, in which suppliers (in this case agencies) flood the market place as demand booms, then, as the buyer (in this case brands) gain more experience and expertise, the market naturally shrinks by around 10 percent, until there is an innovation spike and the market is rejuvenated and the process begins again. In 2012, if you compare the volume of agencies that were started to offer "digital" services against the volume set up in 2009, 2010 and 2011, as well as the volume of agencies that closed, you will see that this "Shakeout" probably took place. So, now the market has begun to mature, where do we go next? We have to innovate, and part of that innovation is becoming more mature in the roll that we see for digital services and integration. The biggest challenge facing businesses today is that the people that have the most experience with social media are (usually) marketers.

This type of advice and consultancy makes it incredibly difficult for a business to think in a truly integrated way—especially outside of the marketing function. For a business to embrace this offline and online convergence effectively, it has to see the wider business context, looking at where social technology can be implemented to create convergent departments across the whole business and understanding the implications and opportunities for cultural change within their organization.

Hopefully, this convergence will signal the death of the "digital" strategy.

In essence, we need to see beyond social technology in marketing. We need to understand that the level of communication, data and insight social technology brings us is having an impact on the whole business (both with consumers and with employees), which asks the question "so what should our digital strategy be then?" Those businesses that share my vision of the future will not have a digital strategy, they will have social thinking and technology in their business's DNA. Social technology will be used to improve the whole business, and these businesses will then be truly social businesses.

It is all well and good me calling time on the "digital" strategy, but how can we move your business forward in a more integrated and innovative way, today? Well there is one more hurdle before we can move onto pragmatic advice, because becoming a social business and using social technology to gather insightful data brings with it a new challenge—complexity.

The next chapter looks at how you can begin to understand how to embrace the complexity that arises from convergence and this mountain of social data, both from a consumer sense, from the point of view of your business's employees and from the point of view of the business itself.

CHAPTER 3

Embracing Complexity

I have always thought that the simplest route to understanding was to break everything into smaller pieces, understand each piece and then slowly put it all back together. Breaking complex systems into manageable, simple blocks. After I failed my Maths A-Level (it is a long story), I started to become quite interested in numbers, and in my first agency job I spent a lot of time looking at how to break down complex systems to create algorithms which produced simple, understandable numbers—the perfect service for clients to purchase, as the concept of social media often terrifies businesses because it feels so big and completely unmanageable.

Simplicity out of complexity, that is what people want, and that is what sells. It is easy to buy something that is very neatly packaged and that seems simple to operate. In fact, (and there are numerous, but as yet unconfirmed theories) that this is how the brain functions—by filing things into metaphorical "boxes."

We see this in society and culture too; taxonomies for our beliefs, our morals, our looks, our friends, our sexuality, our jobs and our possessions. However, we know that life is just not that simple, and things do not tend to fit into categories.

> Categorising always produces reduction in true complexity.
> Nassim Nicholas Taleb, *The Black Swan*

Anyone that has met me in person and stood and spoken to me for more than ten minutes will understand that my whole outlook on life has been shaped by the philosophical and economic theory of *The Black Swan* (and you'll see numerous references to it throughout this book). One of the biggest components of this theory is that we post-rationalize and force things into categories in order for us to be able to understand them within current accepted constructs. Except life, and more importantly in this context, business, is slightly more chaotic and random than our constructs will allow.

There are simply too many variables.

John Maeda is (I think) the father of the simplicity versus complexity debate. His book, *The Laws of Simplicity*, is a manifesto for the importance of simplicity. He explains how simplicity is the process of removing the meaningful from a situation and focussing on that. Creating singularity out of complexity and putting the focus on the core, rather than the periphery. Which is fine, except when we look for the singular meaning, we do so with our internal taxonomies in play. We look for meaning in the known knowns and we cast aside everything else. It is this type of template/category approach that (I personally think) hurts business strategy.

There are very few brands that employ true, unrestricted innovation, but this is human nature, we constantly view new ideas through our old experiences—everything has a personal context by which we judge it. We use empiricism to judge the future, and as Taleb would tell you, just because it has always been, does not make it always so.

The thinking behind *The Black Swan* concept originally came from David Hume, who said "No amount of observations of a white swan can allow the inference that all swans are white, but the observation of a single black swan can refute that conclusion." If we always plan and innovate based on what we have always done, we will never do anything new. Instead we look for simple solutions that we can replicate because they provide comfort and reassurance, and more importantly, from a financial point of view, they provide the potential *for scale*. However, it's important to recognize that there are no templates, because the world is constantly moving. Opinions change, star employees move jobs, the media's political agenda switches, the cultural and social zeitgeist moves on.

What works for one business is never guaranteed to work for the next, and what has worked in one market might not work in the next—and often what has worked in one town is not guaranteed to work in the town next to it. There are too many variables. *Employee experience, customer base, media, economy, culture*—there are simply too many actors on the stage for a one size fits all approach to work. The challenge comes from the fact that a one size fits all approach is easy to buy (and sell) because it creates simplicity out of complexity, comfort out of uncertainty, and branding has traditionally been seen as a way of making these template products and services more desirable—marketing different products benefits at different segments, but for exactly the same product.

You can also see this in the way in which many marketing agencies sell themselves too—they have forgotten why they set up business in the first place (to help brands either make more money or save more money). A huge multinational recently announced in trade media that it was planning on taking ideas from any agency, regardless of what category that agency fell into. It was a revelation. It made the front pages of all of the major trade press titles. Think about this for a moment; *it made the front pages that any agency can have a good idea.* The front page. This is very brave, many brands still define their budgets and work by their agencies, rather than the ideas. While agencies reinforce this in order to stay safe and retain their budgets, they carefully edge their way into categories that get them onto rosters in order to win as much business from the client as possible, and then they become comfortable. "Well we have done some great digital campaigns, if it is not broken, do not fix it."

When thinking about this, I always come back to Taleb. Just because it always has been, does not make it always so. The world is complex and *things change*. Ideas are here and now, and experience was yesterday.

This is a problem with wider business, too. The majority of businesses are eager to scale, so they build departments. Those departments then contain staff who each do a specific job (*very* Adam Smith) and each of those employees is then responsible for their role. Except it is more complicated than that and as the business starts to grow, more and more cracks appear. Everyone absolves themselves of responsibility for the bigger picture, "I do my job to deliver my outputs." There is a culture of micro-business.

These expertise silo's are to be expected in traditional business, you would not expect the head of logistics to be able to write the code for the brand's website, and vice versa, the head of digital is not expected to understand the complexities of supply chain management—a successful business requires people with different skill sets, which is obvious—but as the business grows, scale demands more of those specialized staff. Staff that maybe used to spend one day a week on finances are now expected to spend five days on them, and they become more specialized, where they were once measured on the performance of their whole department (because their scope of work was much broader), they become measured on smaller more specialized jobs. This leads to employees having a three point scale of measurement; the company profits (the ultimate measure is if the business maintains and increases profitability—otherwise they lose their job, the ultimate measure!), their respective departments output (the output of their whole team) and their own output. However, this works on a sliding scale of personal importance—as most are measured by their line manager, who inevitably works in the same department as them, giving a employees a much greater focus on their own output, as someone "more senior" is responsible for the whole department, and someone much more senior is responsible for the whole business. When employees are focused primarily on their own performance, they start to lose sight of the bigger picture. Their skills sets continue to specialize in order to hit those performance measures and anything additional to that skill set becomes of unimportance.

This level of conservatism in business is hurting our organizations, but there are other factors aside from scale. In my opinion, as well as scale and growth, there is also a combination of short-term thinking and fear of failure. The average tenure of a CMO is currently 18–24 months.[1] Usually less than two years. Two years. There is obviously a huge amount of pressure to make an impact in a short amount of time, and so the temptation is to "short" your brand—hit short-term goals at the expense of long-term goals. Then move on with your success to a new job. This is akin to the cartoon strip where the character crosses the lake by stepping quickly over crocodile's nose's—move fast enough and you will not get caught out, stand around waiting and someone will get eaten.

One of the things that John Maeda absolutely nailed was simplicity in branding and communication (he gives a great TED talk on this too—a definite must watch). If human nature prefers to receive information in carefully wrapped packages, sell people products in the same way. The iPhone. Google. Music. Home insurance. Gym memberships. Everything is made as simple as possible in order to make people feel like they are empowered and free (regardless of the complexity that lies behind the facade). But this has led to people "collecting" things. Because brands can produce things en masse that appear simple, people want more things. Social media has also accelerated this. "I can have information neatly packaged and handed to me by Wikipedia immediately, so I want more."

Except that information is much shallower and so we know less about much more.

This short-term, aesthetic approach is fine, until we hit a much bigger issue, at which point we try and rationalize complexity in a dangerous way (see almost any of the media coverage of the London riots in the summer of 2011).

One of my favorite examples of ignorance of these types of constructs and categories is children. Children approach life with such a lack of experience that everything is to be wondered at. In his essay "Painter of Modern Life," Baudelaire said "The child sees everything in a state of newness; he is always *drunk*. Nothing more resembles what we call inspiration than the delight with which a child absorbs form and colour." Those annoying moments when a child continuously asks the question "why?" are always massively revealing, because so frequently we do not have an answer and we answer "because it just is." At what point do we stop (rightly) questioning the world and give in? When do we simply slip beneath the water and look for simple answers?

I think that (for many people) that moment is the moment that their creativity dies. When we give into simplicity and choose the easy life.

Ideas and inspiration come from conflict. It is in clashing ideas that new ideas are born—when our brains drop all of the boxes of categories on the floor of our mind, we finally see something new. That is why the best ideas that we have are out of context—on the bus, in the park, in a restaurant—talking or thinking about something completely out of context (listen to Jon Steel talk about his ideal brand strategist for further proof[2]). Foucault said that inspiration came from the self-destruction and convulsion of our minds—so why do we try and force creativity into a process? If Steven Johnson's idea of the adjacent possible is right, why are not we spending more time destroying the categories we have built in society (and inside our own minds)?

Process is, in my eyes, the antithesis of action. It is like organized fun. Nothing new comes from process, because process is built around empirical constructs. "It has worked before, so it will work again." And it is probably true, if it has worked before, it probably will work again. But it will not achieve the same result, because the world will have moved on since then. Just because it always was does not make it always so.

This also probably goes some way to explain our fear of death. Most people are afraid of death, they cannot comprehend it (unless they have specific religious leanings, in which case they have already simplified death and given it a name) because they have not experienced it before and cannot liken it to anything else (or any other category). Why do we fear death? Because it is inevitable. But why do we not question what existed before we were born? Because surely it is the same? We knew nothing of life before we were born, and we will know nothing of it after we die. Empiricism and simplicity falter at death.

I genuinely believe that we should embrace the chaos. We should rely on our ability to navigate complexity. You just have to look at the work of Hans Monderman and his traffic experiments[3] to see the value and benefit of relying on chaos. Chaos and complexity saves lives because they force people to *think* more. If you cannot buy simplicity, you have to begin to unpick complexity. You are forced into thinking (there is an excellent article on the death of thinking in the *New York Times*[4]).

This type of thinking has to be embraced within business; it stimulates creativity, it forces people to think about the job that they do, the function that their role serves, and how this has an impact on the whole business. By forcing everyone within your business to avoid simplicity, you are going to (1) spark innovation, and (2) highlight the different levels of complexity that have to then be distilled into product development so that we can create simple products and services.

Once we begin to understand the systems and life more intricately, we can begin to accept our limitations, and this has never been so evident than in modern business. The levels of complexity involved in business are mind blowing—every seemingly simple action has a massive knock-on effect (the butterfly effect)—and this is at play both inside and outside the organization.

I believe that there are three types of complexity that we must embrace in business to force creativity and enable simplicity in our output.

CHAOTIC NETWORKS

The people that we employ and the markets that we converse with on a daily basis are made up of complex networks—based on both social (friendships) and interest (shared interest) graphs. As I demonstrated in the chapter on the death of "brand," these networks could give the most ardent sociologist a headache, but they are absolutely fundamental in creating order out of chaos, and the more that we ignore them, the more complex our organizations are going to become.

DATA

The level of data generated through technology is accelerating at a phenomenal pace—in 2010 Eric Schmidt (the then Google CEO) announced that every two days (in 2010) we created more digital data than in the entire lead up to 2003.[5] That's an incredibly complex amount of information to try and devise insights from, but if we can focus our attention on the data that matters, we can use it to drive entire organizations.

THE CONCEPT OF "OPEN BUSINESS" AND LOSS OF CONTROL

If part of accepting complexity is loosening control, then it has come at the perfect time. Social technology, and employee and consumer expectations are forcing businesses to be much more open—while this may sound terrifying to the leadership function, it's incredibly important in becoming closer to both employees and the markets which we wish to sell in and retain as customers.

In the next chapter I will be looking at the huge role that data plays in providing insight and innovation for business, and the level of data and analysis that can be generated from the social web is immense. Arguably more data than business has ever had access to.

CHAPTER 4

The Role of Data

One of the most commonly overlooked aspects that this new world brings is data. From capture, to storage, to analysis and action—how can your organization make the most of all of the social data that is available and relevant to your business? And which of these data are reliable enough to make business decisions based on the insight they provide?

One of the biggest questions for the last few years in business has been how do we collect and manipulate this amount of data into something vaguely informative. Well the convergence of online and offline data has been paralleled by the convergence of offline and online data agencies (For example, Salesforce.com bought Radian6 in 2011) and the ability to start mapping sales to conversations will give us the ability to

- Show return on investment on everything from new propositions to new creative campaigns.
- Allow us to further personalize our work—giving everything the maximum opportunity to resonate with people.
- We will then be able to switch this around and begin to create Single Brand Touchpoints. (SBTs are, as mentioned earlier one of the biggest challenges to brands in a social, reactive world.)

In the new world, where outside connections with consumers are occurring across the whole business, the challenge is that when everyone in the organization is consumer-facing, how do we ensure there is a single brand message? Well, with this new level of data and tracking we will be able to track brand impressions (in both senses) and begin to trace back where each impression has been created—reverse engineering the perception of a brand and looking at where the business needs to focus its attention.

Ultimately, the end result of better data analytics should be increasingly customer-centric strategies, and the way that we reach this more insight-driven world is through Big Data.

Big Data is a term used to reference the vast quantities of data available from the social web. Big Data from a social network such as Facebook could include any of the following:

- Name, date of birth, address, email, mobile phone, IM, website/blog etc.
- Interests and purchase history.
- Social graph (who the individual is friends with, tracked through online connections).

One of the most immediately interesting data sets above is the social graph—as that gives us an idea of the reach of an individual, and also their influence on their social circle—most effectively measured through a process developed by social scientists in the 1960s called Social Network Analysis (which was originally used for tracking the spread of disease among small communities, but is perfectly suited to social platforms as we have the raw data to be able to calculate a number of different things—a basic example of social network analysis can be seen in the chapter on brand versus business). So we can use the connection data and try and build a picture of how people are connected to each other, and then use that to develop a social graph and start to build an accurate picture of how our consumers and employees are connected to one another.

However, the limitations of this type of analysis on its own are numerous, Danah Boyd, one of the senior researchers at Microsoft Research and influential commentator on Big Data, believes that this sort of data is pretty meaningless when you try and compare it to traditional social network analysis (SNA) and traditional sociological theories—as they add a lot more context into the analysis rather than a stand online graph that produces an "articulated network versus a personal network."[1]

Let us take my personal online network as an example; on Facebook I have around 600 friends. Four times the figure that Robin Dunbar believes is manageable. Of those people, I am only in semi-regular contact with about half of my "friends"—and of those, only half would make up any sense of social circle or *influence network* offline. So that would leave me with 150 people within my social graph.

The major risk with this type of standalone analysis is that your data will then show many connections, from old school friends, to people I have met at conferences, none of whom influence anything that I do. So you will end up creating a very diluted social graph for your consumer profiling.

When using Big Data to develop business and consumer insights, context is king.

So, when we begin to combine that social graph data with existing customer insights (from the CRM department), as well as softer data points, such as interests, we can start to build a much fuller consumer profile.

This type of analysis is only going to become more important as businesses become required to be more responsive to customer needs—in fact, in a recent report on Big Data in *The Economist*, Craig Mundie, head of research and strategy at Microsoft said that "Data are becoming the new raw material of business: an economic input almost on a par with capital and labour."[2]

SO WHAT SHOULD YOUR BUSINESS MEASURE?

Since social platforms such as Facebook, YouTube and Twitter have started providing basic insights into usage of their technology, there has been a massive rush of people measuring what I call "vanity metrics." These metrics provide a short-term burst of endorphins for marketing directors and agencies alike; "Hey David, we have got more than 50,000 fans on our Facebook page and the last video we uploaded has more than 100,000 views—we are social media stars!" This is dangerous territory to find yourself in. This type of measurement is *purely* vanity driven and provides little insight into actual behavior, virtually no context into the return on investment of that piece of activity and worse than both of the previous points combined, it lulls the business into a false sense of security, as the business starts to believe its own social media hype, regardless of whether the tills are ringing.

Measurement should be based on core business metrics. As mentioned in previous chapters, if there are clear objectives set for each implementation of social media activity across the business, with a clear strategy, then you can begin to look at how this is measured and what return you see in terms of core business value. For example, if your customer service department starts to resolve customer service issues in forums where customers are expressing concerns and complaining, then the metrics that they should be measured on should reflect those that the "traditional" department is measured on;

- How many issues can you deal with in an hour?
- How many issues are resolved?
- How many issues are escalated?
- How many products are cross-sold?
- Then, it is possible to begin to add in measurements that only apply in the digital space;
- What effect does resolving these issues have on reputation through search engines? (You may find that if there are large groups of people in forums negatively discussing your product or service, that this starts to appear prominently in search engine results when people search for your brand, product or service, so if those problems are resolved, what impact does this have on the first page of search engine results?)
- How many people have responded to your customer service teams post?
- How many people have seen the post?
- How influential is the customer in their social footprint?
- Does the complaint resolution spread to different platforms (IE, if the customer is happy, do they then write about it on their blog or Tweet about it? If so, how many people see this?)

However, these metrics are still effectively secondary business metrics. In this example, the core business metrics that should be being measured are simple.

- How does our customer service function that operates on social platforms effect customer retention?
- How does this activity improve reputation and brand trust?
- Does this activity reduce the overall costs for our customer service department (there is countless whitepapers that highlight that in the time it takes to resolve five customer complaints in a call center, 50 complaints could have been resolved through social platforms—allowing a brand to potentially reduce customer service costs by more than 90%)?

For social activity to be properly integrated into your business, there are three aspects that have to be bullet-proof.

- A set of objectives that match to core business objectives.
- A clear and actionable strategy.
- A measurement and ROI model that is based on the core business objectives identified in the objectives.

Vanity metrics can still play a role in the measurement of activity, but businesses need to understand that they play a small part in building a bigger picture, and that the most important part of activity through social technology is being able to map that data back into insights that the business understands, and preferably that the business is already measuring through "traditional" activity—making the data instantly comprehensible to everyone within the business.

REAL-TIME MEASUREMENT

One of the benefits that social data can bring is real-time measurement and campaign analysis—being able to track metrics such as dwell time, content engagement and seeing which content and activity sparks conversations and sharing gives a decent indication of engagement on a micro-level. When used in conjunction with a measurement and analysis dashboard, it can prove to be incredibly helpful for agile working.

Agile working

It used to be the case that creative, campaigns and ideas would be developed for months at a time in a room held under lock and key, then released into "the wild" and measured on a quarterly or monthly basis through brand trackers—launching activity on social platforms means that this no longer has to be the case and anything that is launched can be done so on a Beta basis. The concept of *agile* is borrowed from programming and development in the software industry, where the theory was developed that by launching when a product was 80 percent complete, a live user base could test it and then tweaks could be made—this, combined with lean production methods (reducing the number of people, processes and barriers to launch involved in a product or service launch) means that the product or service reaches the market much faster and then can be improved while its live—like the ongoing development of Apple's iOS, or Google's PageRank system for delivering search results. As a business, this requires two core components;

- Understanding at a leadership level that products or services do not need to be fully complete before they launch.
- A real-time feedback loop for improvements and modifications.

If agile working can be ingrained into the businesses culture, the products, services and campaigns that the business launches can have improvements made to them over time, at a micro level, increasing reception and engagement with consumers and making people feel as if they are a part of the fabric of the business. This is a true reflection of actually listening to your customers, and reacting to their feedback, in real-time. There are, of course caveats to this, and not every suggestion made needs to be acted on, so whomever is in charge of the feedback loop and reviewing the data needs to understand the context around the suggestions and make educated decisions based on that context. As mentioned in the previous section, it is important to realize the limitations of real-time measurement—it *is not* an indication of overall campaign or product success when dipped into, more an indication of the types of activity or content that are working, so that they can then be tweaked.

The dashboard

Having access to a live dashboard can give a business a massive boost in terms of acting quickly; there are plenty of off-the-shelf products that will help deliver these insights—SalesForce and Omniture both integrate sales information, digital data and social media data into their platforms. However, for those brands that require more customization, I would seriously recommend building a bespoke dashboard—that way reporting, analysis and new types of data that may be unique to your organization can be custom programmed into the dashboard and you can have much greater control of updates to the dashboard.

COMPLEXITY AND ANALYSIS

With this breadth of data available, it's easy to over-analyze, misinterpret or become over-reliant on the insight it provides. In Taleb's *Fooled By Randomness*, he describes how short-term, micro-analysis of stock prices is incredibly dangerous and creates a huge opportunity for mistakes. Imagine opening the *Financial Times* tomorrow morning, finding the list price for Coca-Cola and making a judgment on the whole company, its history and its future based on that single figure. It lacks context, yet this is how social media data is being used by businesses all over the world every day. I have been privy to numerous meetings with businesses where a digital agency has used changes in social data (such as sentiment, or peaks in "fans") to justify fundamental changes to how the business is positioning itself online—most commonly, these types of conversations happen in what people like to describe as a "social media crisis."

As businesses and employees become more experienced with social technology, this is type of scaremongering is becoming less common, however the ambulance chasers still prevail and use the smallest of excuses to engage with a brand and help it to "sort out the crisis." Mostly these crises are taken vastly out of context; usually a few complaints on a brand's Facebook page is seen as a crisis, even when the said brand sells hundreds of thousands of products every day—again, context is king. Rushing into brash decisions based on a few complaints or a change in sentiment about your brand across the web is dangerous and can provoke a much bigger change in attitude from the thousands of customers that are happy.

"Sentiment"

One of the most misused social metrics is sentiment. In theory, social media monitoring tools that measurement sentiment will give you an indication of the overall sentiment around a set of keywords (most frequently your brand name, to reflect how people feel about your brand online), however, the technology behind these metrics is severely limited, with error rates ranging from 40 percent to 80 percent—making accurate analysis virtually impossible. Currently, most tools will look through the social web for mentions of your keywords, then analyze the other words used in close proximity to your keyword. So, for example, if you were looking for mentions of "Gatorade," the tool would analyze the sentiment of ten words either side of the mention and make a calculation based on those words as to the sentiment of the mention. The main issue being that vernacular is complex—sarcasm, irony and profanity confuse systems like this and more often than not (40%–80% of the time) the measure is incorrect.

Even with advanced computational methods of analysis such Bayesian Analysis (usually used to filter spam in email programs), Markov Chains (a very complicated method that you can use to help computers learn) or even Support Vector Machines (how "premium" monitoring companies "teach" their computers to learn) there are still massive flaws with computers trying to understand what we mean when we publish content online. Plus, when I say "I love Washington," do I mean the location, the actor (Denzel) or the cake? Or a friend of mine? Or a TV program?

The other problem is that our opinions and sentiment are transient. We're allowed to change our minds and we frequently do (some of us more than others) and if our content is going to be analyzed, how do we do that? Do we create aggregate compound sentiment scores? Or do we display individual mentions? There are too many variables and potential complications for a computer, or most humans, to understand.

The only true way to measure sentiment is to purchase a technology that uses regular manual analysis (literally a group of social analysts who spend hundreds of painstaking hours analyzing each mention to manually score it for sentiment—the quantitative approach) or, alternatively, speak directly to those connected to the business (industry influencers, employees, customers, potential new customers) and take a much more qualitative approach. My personal recommendation is to use a combination of both, as the former has become much more cost effective through tools like Amazon's Mechanical Turk and the latter helps to build stronger relationships with the community and a much more open business environment.

Again, it is important to put everything into context, understand the limitations of the technology and only measure the things that make a difference to your business.

CONTEXT

There are a myriad of factors involved in the way in which a business performs and is perceived—from the media agenda, and the cultural zeitgeist to the weather, and changes to the ways in which people access information on your business. Trying to wrap all of this context into your analysis of data can be a nightmare, especially when most of the supporting information is difficult to compute—we are reminded of Bachelier's quote from his *Theorie de la Speculation*.

> The factors that determine activity on the Exchange are innumerable, with events, current or expected, often bearing no apparent relation to price variation. Beside the somewhat natural causes for variation come artificial causes: The Exchange reacts to itself, and the current trading is a function, not only of prior trading, but also of it is relationship to the rest of the market.

When this level of complexity is presented, it makes context, analysis and prediction impossible to calculate. What the business can do, however, is work across different parts of the organization to pull all relevant context into the dashboard—so for example, having an RSS feed from the stock exchange and Reuters will provide additional context to data, while also having media monitoring across competitor activity will give a broader context to the data still. To narrow down the context, it is important to be presented with all information available, but it is also incredibly important to understand what cannot be measured, the "known unknowns" and then also to allow for "unknown unknowns." By looking at the context of organizational data in this way, we are taking a much broader approach, but giving the business the best opportunity to react quickly to changes in the market and consumer behavior.

INTERNAL SOCIAL DATA

There are three sets of important data that can be collected from an internal communications point of view; email logs (based on whom is emailing whom, and at what frequency), social media information from employees, and measuring internal perceptions of the business and brand (a more formal version of the suggestion box—which I will go into further detail on later in the book).

Email social network analysis

As previously explored, one of the biggest steps to creating Single Brand Touchpoints is to understand how your employees connect with one another inside the business, below the traditional hierarchical model imposed by the business itself. One reliable way to do this is to analyze who emails who (careful; not the content of the email, the frequency of which people email each other) and begin to build a social graph that shows the true relationships within your business. This data can then be used to understand how messaging moves between departments, who your influential employees are and how you can group teams together to get increase efficiency and happiness (through combining mixed skill sets and friendship groups).

SOCIAL MEDIA INFORMATION FROM EMPLOYEES

One of the most frequent questions that comes up when talking to a business interested in understanding social media is how do we get our employees talking on our behalf more frequently. This is exciting to hear as an agency, as the latent knowledge inside the business is incredibly powerful, yet often difficult to trace and analyze. If a business can understand which of its employees are talking in which spaces online and about what, they can then begin to work *with* them to build stronger connections to the world outside of the business. For example, I had a meeting with a new client recently, and through a small amount of desk research, we found that a number of its research and development team frequently write blog posts on their work (sans sensitive information, fortunately) and the whole team were active on Twitter, using the network to speak to other people in the industry—which is fantastic, and should not be feared by the business. If you can engage your employees and understand who holds significant influence (across any area) you can start to do a number of things;

- Explore the concepts of the Adjacent Possible mentioned in an earlier chapter (if the CEO is interested in exploring a new market and an employee that works in HR has particular expertise in that space, they can add significant value to the decision making process).
- A business can begin to explore the connections that its employees have, looking at their social graphs and understanding how this information can be used to gather more social information and build better products and services.

■ From an internal communications perspective, the business can begin to build a much more rounded picture of its employees— understanding more about their motivations and interests.

Three incredibly powerful ways of increasing employee engagement, through a simple collection of social data.

Measuring internal perceptions

The business suggestion box is an age old concept, but there are many modern adaptations of this that allow employees to feel like they can make a real difference to the business (and be rewarded for it), while also allowing the business to capture data on internal perceptions of the business. From simple data collection such as "what does our brand stand for?" to more detailed questions such as "how do you feel our last service proposition performed, and why"? Simple questions, carried out in an open way using social technology can reap real rewards.

SEARCH DATA

Over the last six years, I would say the most useful data for understanding human insights I have encountered has been the data that can be *freely* obtained from search engines. With Google being used by more than 80 percent[3] of the world's Internet users, it gives a pretty robust sample size from its search insights and analytics, and the types of inferences that you can make through its two primary tools (Google AdPlanner and Google Trends) can be combined with data from almost every department at your business.

Google AdPlanner

The AdPlanner tool is intended to be used to help target high-volume keyword searches and low-competition advertising space, but equally it can be used as a tool for understanding how people search for your brand or product. It will help explain the types of additional words that people use when searching (as most people have become used to long tail search strings such as "smartphone 4G HD screen" as opposed to just "smartphone"), it will also help highlight simple nuances in search behavior, such as using the incorrect spelling of your brand or products. I spent six months on secondment with a research agency a few years ago working on a social project with Kellogg's and the volume of people that searched for Keloggs far outweighed those that could correctly spell the brand name—this impact that this has is that the brand in question has to start collecting data from additional keywords, to ensure that all content is being collected (regardless of spelling mistakes).

The AdPlanner tool can also be used to figure out where influential communities are around your brand, that might not be specifically referencing your brand. Using broad category terms as keywords, the tool will display related terms, which you can then use to create a much broader keyword list to input into your social media monitoring tool—which will quickly uncover a whole raft of new, influential communities that simple searches would not have discovered initially.

Google Trends

Trends provides a timeline of search traffic to certain keywords, so you can input a number of terms and it will display a graph that shows search volumes over time—which is particularly useful for tracking crises or new product launches. It provides an additional level of insight into public relations activities (if the campaign has been successful, there should be a peak in search behavior around the launch) and it also tries to connect influential pieces of content that were published around the same time to add additional insight into the increase in search traffic. One way in which I have used this service before has been for watching rising trends, combining search data with increased activity across Twitter and Facebook—so as a trend starts to take off, if you can correlate search volumes to conversations on social platforms, you can begin to plan content and ideas in a truly agile way—reacting live to consumer behavior.

THE CHIEF DATA OFFICER

So, with all this data flooding into your organization, how should it be managed? How should your business give it context, understand it and then take action based on it?

Welcome to the rise of the Chief Data Officer (CDO).

If Microsoft's Craig Mundie is correct, then over the next ten years data is going to become an invaluable resource, and the source of most of it is going to come from insights gained through a mix of social technology and traditional data sources such as CRM and focus groups. This may sound didactic, but no business can afford to ignore the data available, it is going to help every business transition from the old world of creating products en masse and then using advertising and marketing to create differentiation, to, as John Willshire, of the innovation consultancy Smithery says, "Make things people want, not make people want things." This role should sit neatly alongside the existing positions of Chief Information Officer (CIO) and Chief Technology Officer (CTO) as all three need to work together to produce the most efficient system to deliver data into the organization, however, the CDO will be responsible for external and internal data management from a more insight-driven position than the CIO, who is role is usually much more focused on the technical aspects of data and IT.

The Chief Data Officer should be responsible for the following:

- Presenting data back at a board/leadership level.
- Working closely with the CIO and/or CTO to develop information flows and technologies.
- Collection of data from all sources, both across the business and externally.
- Procurement or development of the dashboard.
- Analysis and translation of the data in tangible information.
- Reporting data back across the whole business, ensuring that the data is appropriate for each audience.
- An comprehensive understanding of the accuracy of metrics.
- An understanding of the development of new measurement technology and machine-based learning systems.

CONCLUSION

Once your organization begins to integrate social technology into different departments, the flow of data between them needs to be managed, and analysis needs to be standardized, so that each insight that is derived from the data is of the same quality—and this process needs to be managed by a senior analyst (CDO). There is already a raft of information flooding into your organization, but the process that I have outlined above will help to structure it and add additional raw information from social platforms into it. Even simple steps like combining existing information in the CRM system with simple social data should see an immediate impact—imagine the improvement it would make to the customer experience if conversations could easily flow from a platform like Twitter into the call center, completely fluidly? Or if your product managers were having in-depth conversations with a journalist on a forum and that conversation then lead to the journalist visiting the research and development labs to trial new products and give immediate feedback? This type of data flow and communications is not going to happen overnight, but it will help your business move forward into the converged age, providing unparalleled insights into your market and helping to build stronger relationships with those outside of the walls of your business.

That is the business of the future.

The theory, ideas and tools I have outlined above have all worked in practice, with global clients, but what I have found has been the most efficient way to integrate these new data sets into a business is by creating a working group of people from across the business that understand analytics (both traditional digital analytics from tools like Omniture, as well as social analytics from tools such as SalesForce.com) and working together to help identify what can be measured, what each department would benefit from and then developing a strategy toward achieving this goal. With the right group of people (that you could potentially recruit through running the email log network analysis) it is going to be possible to take the data locked away inside and outside the business and provide real, raw insights that the business can only benefit from. The key thing to remember is context; in terms of additional data, not over-simplifying complex data and combining everything with wider business information.

CHAPTER 5

An Introduction to Social Business

So, in the previous chapters we've looked at how this new world has redefined the role of the business and its increasing importance over the role of the brand, how consumer and employee convergence between online and offline worlds is reshaping business, and how embracing complexity within your organization can help to create a much more simple business proposition—if done correctly—but what name do we give to this new type of business? Well, in my mind, this new type of business is simply called a social business.

Firstly, let us clear up any potential confusion that may arise based on the term "social business," as there's often confusion about whether the prefix "social" is in relation to technology, people or corporate responsibility. My definition (which is by no means definitive, but for the purpose of the next 60,000 words it would probably be much easier if we both know what I'm talking about when I mention it) of social business is:

> Social business: a business that has human insight in its DNA, enabled by technology.

The definition seems simple enough, in fact every business in existence could probably class itself as a social business, as being social is about communicating and communication is fundamental to the operation of a business. However, the way in which that communication takes place, and how we communicate outside of our business has fundamentally changed and while all businesses could call themselves social, few could claim that they have human insight built into their DNA.

Technology makes this easier.

Technology enables everyone within the business to communicate with everyone else, both inside and outside of the business, and this is fundamental to driving innovation and retaining customers. In our hyper-connected world, this is already taking place, it is just that often the leadership function does not know it is taking place, or understand how to utilize it and use it to increase profitability, innovation and customer satisfaction. In the last book that I contributed to in 2011,[1] I highlighted three issues that stand in front of businesses today, and all three remain pertinent 18 months on. Those three issues are:

- Increasingly empowered consumers and employees.
- Businesses operating in silos.
- A lack of organizational agility or adaptiveness.

The past ten years has seen social technology provide a huge increase in the reach and scale of communication that individuals have—and as you can see from the chapter on embracing convergence, this new type of dynamic network is getting stronger as people become much more comfortable with technology playing such an active role in their lives. We are not necessarily becoming more social, it is just that our social lives are becoming more visible because they are being documented and played out live, online. This is having a dramatic impact on the reach of word of mouth—the hyper-connectivity of weak tie networks also means that where we once used to reach smaller, stronger networks, we can now reach the same strong networks, but we can also reach much wider networks too. Simple online conventions like sharing Facebook statuses, retweeting tweets, or linking to a blog post give the six degrees of separation a huge accelerator effect.

The effect that this has on businesses is obviously evident; a negative or positive experience that was once confined to the small network of friends we held can now travel around the world in a matter of seconds. Consumers have become empowered by this technology, the ability to share experiences of products and services with their peers means that there is now much more accountability put on the business. While businesses are fundamentally built on communication, this has, traditionally, been a very one-way, broadcast relationship—communicating information one way, en masse. However, now businesses are being forced to become much more open, transparent and *social*.

In the following nine chapters I'm going to explore how your business can become more social across multiple disciplines—not just marketing, but the *whole* business (and feel free to skip the chapters that are not quite right for you, this is not intended to be a novel, instead more of a text book that you can dip into when the time is right). I'll be exploring the role that social technology can play over the following business departments and disciplines:

- Leadership (including strategic shifts that need to be made, strategy and planning, corporate control, culture, acquisitions, scaling and growth, competitor insights, new markets, and supplier strategy)
- Marketing (including the case against campaigns, integrated marketing strategy, planning, creative, media buying, your business's website, search engine optimization, in-store marketing, mobile and experiential)
- Public relations (including modern media relations, blogger relations, understanding newsflow online, investor relations, public affairs and advocacy, public information, spin, transparency and Wikipedia, corporate social responsibility, reputation management, and crisis communications)
- Sales (including customer acquisition, cross-selling, customer journey and experience, mobilizing the sales force, and channel strategy)
- Research and development (including research, new product development, competitor research, sourcing expertise, human insights, "Labs" powered by social technology, identifying common product/service flaws, testing and trials, crediting the community, open source your products, and understanding how to scale social technology)
- Human resources (including employee conversation guidelines, social business mentoring schemes, workshops and training, monitoring, feedback and evaluation, internal communications, collaboration, change, crowdsourcing, community, communications flow, recruitment, and IT)
- Customer service (including getting started, recruitment and training, monitoring, regulation, channels, escalation process, internal integration, scalability and cost savings, amplification of resolutions, and social customer relationship management).

So, let's explore how your business can become a truly social business. The first step, and the next chapter, is about strategic shifts that are going to have to be made by the business's leadership function before the organization can move toward becoming a social business.

CHAPTER 6

Leadership

Building a social business is not about having a Twitter or Facebook strategy, it is about stitching back together the constituent parts of your business that have become silo'd and disparate over the course of its history to create a fluid entity that allows data and insights to flow freely across every department of your business. Social business is about relinquishing corporate control, and building an open culture, where anyone within your organization can make suggestions and improve the performance of your business. It is about actually listening to and understanding your market, not from behind a camera listening to twelve people discuss what they do and don't like about your products or services, but about being present at 4 a.m. when a mother is asking a forum of her peers what to do because her washing machine has broken and it is leaking water throughout her home. Social business is about getting so close to your market that they feel like a part of your business, because they are, your market is your business. Without them all you have is a building full of people in starchy suits showing presentations filled with graphs pointing optimistically upwards and making predictions about "what our core demographic" wants. These presentations are unnecessary, because your "core demographic" is telling you what they want, what they need, what they hate and why they hate it, it is just that your organization is not listening to them. Becoming a social business is about stepping back out from behind your desk and engaging with your employees, trusting them, encouraging them and making them feel like they are part of something much bigger than a nine to five. The world has fundamentally changed over the last twenty years—we are in a time of economic uncertainty when people cannot afford to take risks on products or services that might not work, but fortunately for consumers technology came to the rescue, giving them access to their peers like they had never know before. Those peers are leaving reviews of your business on TripAdvisor and pointing out that "while the description said it was in the middle of the city, it was actually a thirty minute walk." They are tweeting about your rude customer service team. They are "Liking" your Facebook page to get the discount voucher and then immediately "Unliking" your page because they do not want their 2000 friends to think that they were endorsing your brand. The world has changed, and it is time for your business to change to.

In this new world corporate control is seen as overbearing by everyone except "the board," but that is ok, because your employees are circumventing your firewalls and breaking your rigid "brand guidelines" everyday, between nine and five. They are doing this because they are consumers too, and their online and offline worlds have collided, and they can see the benefit of building empathy with the market by speaking to people as humans and that handing over the company "secret sauce" builds trust because it takes away the feeling of corporate secrecy. It does not matter that you think that "that social media is just a fad," or that you see the Facebook IPO as the biggest sign yet that we are in the throes of another dot-com bubble—there are nearly one billion people using Facebook to connect with friends, family and businesses that they love, one in six people in the UK are sending 140 character messages to each other, and they are talking about the latest celebrity gossip, the state of the current UK government, and that mobile that they bought six months ago that has all of a sudden stopped working. Social media is bigger than your business, but that is not to say that it is not having a fundamental effect on it.

Now is the time to act, to empower your employees, to listen to your market and to accept the complexity that technology has brought to your door.

There are ten fundamental tenets that need the business leadership needs to focus on to begin the process becoming a social business and stopping your business from being run by employees who do not care, trying to sell commoditised, undifferentiated products and services to people that do not want them. Just ten, and I will make a promise, and the leadership function will like this; if you integrate social technology into the heart of your business you will reduce operational costs, increase agility and responsiveness, help create truly innovative products and increase both acquisition and retention figures. So, those tenets.

- **Focus on data**
- Feed your organization with social data from customers, the data is your market.
- Data is not just external, use data to better understand your workforce.
- Keep the data flowing, that way your organization is always on, always learning.

Data is, as outlined earlier in this very book, the future of your business. It is the reason that Amazon has created a billion dollar company in a (relatively) short amount of time, it is the reason that Nike created Nike+, and it is the reason that Gatorade launched its "Mission Control" room for tracking social data and digital analytics. The level of access that we have to data through social and digital technologies ensures that we never have to produce a product or service on "gut instinct" again—sure, the role of gut instinct will always be important, but now we can test the instinct, we can back it up and we can introduce the product of our gut instinct to the right people, at the right time.

Feed your organization with social data from customers, and you can trust the data, it is not from a sample size of a few thousand people, rather it is from a sample size of your entire market.

IT'S THE MARKET DATA

So-called Big Data has been a big focus for many businesses for the last ten years, but few are implementing it across the business, with many organizations struggling to standardise the data to let it move freely from department to department. Another key area of growth is going to be internal data—not just sales and performance data, but understanding how your employees talk to each other, who influences who, and how you can use this insight to improve staff happiness and boost efficiency and innovation.

Pulling in the right data, analyzing not what you can, but what you should, and hiring a Chief Data Officer will enable you to match data from all over your business to core business metrics—integrated measurement of this scale and breadth is complex, but the insight that it provides will make your business unparalleled in your market. This data then allows you to start accurately benchmarking your activity, not based on flimsy statistics from individual departments, but from the whole of your business—highlighting areas of potential growth, potential problems and improvements and recommendations for innovation.

However, one important thing to remember is that conversations and opinions can be transient, so focus on keeping the data flowing into your organization—have a micro-view, but analyze the data on a macro basis. It will enable your whole business to be more reactive and agile, and spot trends and potential new opportunities, giving you a serious competitive edge over other businesses.

- Focus on being reactive
- Listen to your market, learn how it moves and who influences it and then react to the changes.
- Customer feedback does not always need to be implemented, but it should always be listened to.
- Cut down research and development time by using social data and testing, and create lean teams that are prepared to launch beta products.

One of the core benefits of becoming a social business is being able be agile and responsive to your market—the market moves quickly, tastes change, but if you can understand the network dynamics of your business, both internally and externally, your organization is going to be in a much stronger position to understand what has changed, why it has changed, how it effects your business and how to react to the changes. Understanding the influence that certain people have over these networks will help—these people need to be paid particular attention to as they set the agenda, spread messages and information quickly, and they can be massively useful in predicting trends and swings in opinion and sentiment.

Throughout this book I have talked about listening as a core component of any social business, however, you will notice at no point have I decreed that every snippet of feedback should be acted upon, because it should not. Listen to what people think about your products and services, but knee-jerk reactions to niche opinions and statements might disrupt an otherwise content majority of the market. There is a difference between being lead by the consumer to arrive at what can only be described as a Frankenstein product or service that satisfies no consumer need (see the episode of The Simpsons in which Homer designs a new concept car for his brother) and using market insights to carefully select improvements to products and services and new products to create greater value and have a much bigger impact on the experience that the market has with your business.

This type of reactive business has many benefits, but one of the core benefits is the ability to reduce the overheads in the research and development department, driving innovation, and launching and improving products and services at much faster rate than ever before. This can be through using social data to concept new ideas, or testing new propositions using social focus groups—but whatever the specific use, the important part of this type of activity is being able to *react*. Data on its own, without any follow on is useless—it has to have an impact—and for this to have the desired impact, research and development teams have to be lean, agile, and the business needs to be prepared (and be able communicate clearly externally and internally) to launch beta products—the promise to all concerned being that these products and services will evolve and improve through constant iteration and innovation.

Having a clear process flow from receiving live data, to analysis, to action—smooth working across departments and lean teams will help to increase the velocity of this process—being a reactive business is about reacting to the right things, at the right time, in the right way. You need to cut corporate bureaucracy if this is to happen—if a market is moving particularly quickly, the last thing that your business needs is either death by PowerPoint or to face the committee firing squad before a decision can be made. Plan for speed, by being lean and removing unnecessary barriers to market.

Everything is changing all the time; trends, data, market needs, cultural zeitgeist, stock prices, employees, politics. Embrace the constant state of flux in business, the market and your employees and trust change. You can prepare for change by knowing what you do know, and knowing what you don't know, but sometimes you don't know what you don't know.

If your business is agile and responsive it is going to keep you ahead of your competitors and it will keep you in the heads of your consumers. Focus on being a great business for your employees and your market, here and now. Forget yesterday, complexity brings with it an atmosphere for change, so embrace today.

- **Focus on people**
- Your business is your people, whether they are your employees or your market. Give them your attention.
- Create the right culture and your business will feel like a movement—both employees and the market will defend you and protect you.
- Understand networks of people, how messages and information move within them, how they change and how you can be part of them.

This is arguably one of the most important tenets to building a successful social business. Businesses are founded on communication—the way in which we communicate our vision, culture and products to our employees has a massive effect on the way in which they communicate them to the market—but also, the way in which the market communicates its understanding of the business and its products *back* to the business is equally important, and the one constant in this process is *people*. Your people, be them internal or external, are your business. They make everything happen, they buy your products and services, and they talk to their networks about what they think of your business. Traditionally, "the corporation" has been a construct that moved the focus away from people and onto this metaphysical creation—social business brings the focus back firmly onto the people. Without them, your business will not exist, so pay them the attention that they deserve. Listen to them.

If you can, as a leader of your business, create the right culture, you can make your business feel like a collective of people, both internally and externally, working together to create more meaning from your products and services. "We are all in this together, to live easier, faster, more enjoyable lives"—this is the type of sentiment that your business should be looking to generate by focusing on the people. Everyone involved in your business, both the market and your employees, should feel like they are involved in something bigger than a business, it should feel like a movement—people should feel emotional when they discuss your business, then giving them information about your brand becomes an entertaining process, rather than an arduous sell to someone without any emotional connection.

Ask yourself, when was the last time you "Liked" a business page on Facebook that you had little emotional connection to? Exactly.

The way in which you can start to focus on people is by listening, delivering on your promises and promise better things to come—exciting and embedding employees and the market into the fabric of your business.

The networks that we discussed earlier in the book will help your business to start to understand how people effect your organization—identifying which network's "touch" your business, who is active within them, who is influential within them and how messages and information move across them will help you and your business understand how to be *part* of them. Far too many businesses take the arrogant approach of forcing their way into conversations and communities, with total disrespect for the people that drive those conversations—listen to your people, act in a humble manner and add value. That is how a social business should behave.

- **Focus on retention**
- If your business can keep its customers happy, they will become more embedded. They will tell your brand story, they will tell their friends about your products and services.
- Not only is it cheaper to keep staff happy, but they will also build a much stronger bond with your business—having a revolving door will damage your SBTs.
- The best acquisition strategy is a good retention strategy—cut churn, improve satisfaction, and boost profitability.

A few months ago, I was talking to Graham, the creative director at VCCP Share, and we were discussing the role of social technology in retaining customers—and he used the phrase "The best acquisition strategy is a great retention strategy." By focusing on keeping your existing customers happy, your business will obviously improve customer satisfaction and cut the customer churn rate, but more importantly (and more subtly), those happy customers will become advocates for your business. They will talk about your products and services with their friends, they will talk about the fantastic customer service they received upon finding a problem, or detail how they worked alongside your research and development team to make modifications to a service that they saw opportunities for improvement with. These people will drive your acquisition strategy and, as I am about to detail in the following chapters, the different departments of your business can then use this advocacy to capture leads much more effectively than cold calling and mass sales messaging.

Social platforms and consumer empowerment ensures that this positive word of mouth spreads through networks quickly—reaching far more people with a trusted message (from peer-to-peer, rather than business-to-consumer) than your organization could ever hope to reach. A simple tweet about a great customer service experience can, in very few steps, be seen by millions of people, each of those people seeing your social business in action and lifting consideration at the same time. Deliver fantastic products, and fantastic service to your existing customers and they will stay. Help them to tell their friends, and their friends will join too.

Turn your existing customers into business advocates through great service, adding value and creating relationships with them through your employees—and this can this can be achieved through relatively simple means; empower your employees to really *talk* to the market, train them properly to deliver a fantastic customer experience, and, as a business, *give* to your customers—it is, after all, much cheaper to retain a customer than it is to acquire a new customer (in some cases it is five times more expensive to acquire a new customer, than retain an existing one—yet if you retain more customers and encourage them to talk about products and services, the cost of acquisition falls even further!).

Never lose focus on your customers—they power your business through buying your products and services, feeding you the invaluable data that drives your business, and providing you with a constant source of live feedback.

Your existing customers are a key element on your journey to better products and services, new customers and a reduction in customer churn and acquisition costs.

■ **Focus on being open**
■ An open business is not some Silicon Valley idealistic, beanbags-in-reception type approach, it is allowing skills, expertise, and data to flow (unrestricted) through your business. The best people, and the best data, for the job.
■ Allow your market, your influencers and your critics into your business—they can only make it better. Open business is about transparency and honesty.

■ Stop pushing your "brand" and focus on delivering your "business"—a brand voice can sound disingenuous and corporate, giving your employees a voice will let the market see the humans inside your business.

The term "open business" has been used by marketing and management consultants in shiny suits for decades—the concept sold is usually around having "hot desks" and open plan offices, in order to drive a culture of being an "open business." For me, being open as a business is much more literal. It is about letting your business live and breathe as an organism, it is about autonomy and integration across different departments, allowing people to work in mixed-expertise groups to collaborate on ideas and projects, breaking down departmental silos and standardising data to allow data and insights to flow between different teams in different departments, it is about giving people the freedom to see *the whole* business, and letting the *whole business* see them, allowing for much greater understanding of business vision, the roles and responsibilities of different departments and understanding the different skill-sets and expertise across the whole business. It is most certainly *not* about posters in the bathrooms filled with empty-sounding promises and pre-meditated job-swaps once every 12 months. If your business can master this, it can become an open, social business, and you will see the benefits almost immediately.

However, this is not just about the inner-workings of your organization—it is also about being open to the outside world. Your most vocal critics can be your most useful tool, so bring them into the fabric of your business, let them speak to the customer service team leader, show them your product or service development roadmap for the next 12 months—*trust them*. Transparency and honesty is key to being open—and secretive businesses prompt suspicion and investigation, people wonder what a business has to hide. More importantly, let your market and those that influence them into your business—let them speak directly to the managing director, give them information that they cannot find anywhere else, tell them how your business works—the worst that can happen is that they tell other people, in which case your business story becomes widely known. Do not worry about losing competitive advantage by being open—if you are using social data from your market and driving innovation through each and every component of your business, you have nothing to lose and trust, understanding and loyalty to gain.

Avoid the common trappings of corporate speak and press release regurgitation—people buy people, they don't buy faceless corporations that hide behind shiny stock imagery and stationary. If you can create a culture that is human and open, your employees can talk to the market with a voice that it trusts, a voice that's honest. Humans make mistakes, they say the wrong thing, and they make bad decisions, but people forgive them because they are human. Your business does not need a single point of view, it needs thousands of them, from your employees, united by a single theme—and that single theme should be your businesses mission statement.

Overall, great relationships build great businesses; be more open as an organization and put all your focus on building great relationships with your employees, your market and your partners, and the great business will follow.

- ▪ **Focus on culture**
- ▪ Culture cannot be created, it must be guided and it can only come from your employees—having training days paintballing is a sticking plaster on your organization's culture, fix the fundamentals.
- ▪ Your culture needs to reflect your ambition to be a social business—let people talk to each other, learn from each other and enjoy what they do.
- ▪ If you follow these tenets, you are more likely to create a culture of pride—when people work to create products and services that make people's lives better, they feel proud of what they do.

Culture is another of those terms that has become embedded in the vocabulary of over-excited management consultants for a long time now, but it is an incredibly important aspect of creating a social business. The culture that you try to guide your organization toward has to come from the way in which the leadership function behaves, and how you structure your business for change. Culture comes from the collective understanding of your employees and the market of your business vision—but this is not delivered through a weekly mail-merged email, it has to be embedded in every word and action that your business carries out. Your people need to *see* that your business is becoming a social business for it to become a social business. By following the processes I have outlined throughout this book, your business can become more social, but you have to communicate this and demonstrate it wholeheartedly for that to become ingrained in your organization's culture. A simple rebrand to "organization2.0" is not going to convince your own employees, let alone your market, that anything has changed. A board of suits do not create a culture, the people that it employees do. Share your vision with your employees and they'll share it with you and with the market and with their friends and with anyone that will listen. Demonstrate positive change.

This is obviously harder than it sounds, changing your corporate culture is never going to happen overnight, but then this book is about long-term success, not get-rich-quick Ponzi schemes. Communicate the changes that are going to be taking place, explain how the organization will be moving forward, show the difference that this will make and your employees will feel the change. The point that I made earlier about creating the same sense that a movement has is how that culture is born—and if you can follow the route to that sense of "oneness," letting people discuss the changes and improvements, opening up the organization, and breaking down the barriers of the business, people will start to take pride in what they are involved in—whether that is employees or the market, people will want to promote their association with your business. They will feel a sense of achievement in making people's lives better.

Then, and only then, will a culture of social, open business breed through your offices and market place. However, the impact that this will have will be incredible—everyone will feel like they are working toward something much bigger, they will feel like the role that they play in the success or failure of this change is fundamental—people will feel like they are the change, and this will have a huge impact on whether or not your objective of becoming a social business is achieved. Build a culture around these ten tenets and your business will become truly social—driving innovation, customer acquisition and cutting costs. The bottom line of your finance sheet depends on this cultural shift, so do not take it lightly or leave it until the last minute.

- ▪ **Focus on innovation**
- ▪ Your business is only as good as its last product and every time you get ahead of the game, another business is going to be working harder to beat you—never stop innovating.

■ The opportunity for innovation can come from anywhere or anyone, but it has to be granted to employees through culture and trust. Trust your employees.

■ If your organization gets complacent and stops listening to the market, you will lose market share, you will lose your best employees and, ultimately, you will fail.

Innovation is what keeps the market moving forward. It used to be that innovation was thought to exist in a vacuum, with white-coated research and development employees sitting in laboratories for weeks on end creating "new and improved" versions of your product and services lines—but that is not the case anymore. Research and development has moved outside of the lab and into the everyday work place, and those sparks of genius are no longer just coming from your research and development team, but from every employee and from the market itself. Ideas are not the preserve of the creative classes and, if history teaches us anything, it is that great ideas can come from anywhere. From the perspective of your business, this is a great situation to be in as the market is becoming more and more demanding on products and services meeting their needs—and these needs change. The complexity in today's markets means that a simple change in dynamic can signal the need for change across an entire product line overnight—and if your business is reactive and agile, these new needs can be met. Just because something is the way that it is today, does not guarantee that it will be the same tomorrow. Things change and empirical evidence stands for nothing when your market share goes into decline—nobody cares that your business was "the world's leading" yesterday.

ACT LIKE A SHARK, NEVER STOP MOVING FORWARD

This notion of the need for constant innovation, coupled with the fact that ideas can, and should, come from all over your business is of positive benefit to your business. Creating a culture of innovation and openness, and trusting your employees to work outside of their own departments on problems will fuel efficiency and creativity.

Innovation is not limited to the research and development team's work on new products and services either; innovation should span your whole business, from the way in which pay checks are printed, to the production of new logos—innovation has to be systematic across your whole organization for it to truly make a difference. Promote a culture of involvement and your employees will give you these great ideas because they understand how your business works and they want to be involved in the success of your organization, they want to feel like they are making a difference.

I will go on to talk about it in more detail in Chapter 10, but you can, and should, involve your market innovation. The people that buy, use and review your products and services everyday will give you great ideas because they understand how your products and services work—they know what your business stands for, and they know how to make it better, because these types of innovation make their lives easier and them more likely to maintain loyalty to your business.

Having a lean and agile business culture means that you can constantly tweak the formula to your business as well as your products and services—and by promoting honesty and transparency, you stem the potential negatives of getting things wrong—talk about trying to make improvements with your employees, the market and those that influence the market and they will appreciate your efforts. All in all, just try new things. The worst that can happen is that your business can just go back to the old formula, at best your business can improve on something everyday—driving sales and satisfaction with it.

If your business becomes complacent about its products and services, change will leave you behind, as will your competitors. Never stop innovating and use the data and insights that will (by now) be flowing through your organization to drive this. A business that focuses on being reactive to its market and employees is a business that is constantly looking to improve—if your business is agile enough to react fast enough, both your market and employees will remain content.

Remember, innovation does not happen between nine and five— embrace the always on culture—be flexible with your employees and they will constantly be on. Be flexible with your market and they will constantly be yours.

COMPLACENCY KILLS COMPANIES

- **Focus on integration**
- If your business is going to be open and innovative, that is going to involve breaking down your organization's silos.

■ Integration is not just about internal communications, it is also about integrating with your market. Find your business's role in the market.

■ Great ideas are not the preserve of the creative—creativity is everywhere, you just need to promote integration to unlock it.

Throughout this book (specifically in the next six chapters) integration plays a major role. If you want to become an outwardly social business, you must first increase the "socialness" of your business on the inside, and integration across departments, collaborative working, and trusting your employees to contribute to any business problem is absolutely core to achieving your objectives.

There are three parts of traditional corporate culture that need to broken down before organizational integration can really take shape; (1) hierarchy—your employees need to feel comfortable discussing anything with anyone across your whole organization, by creating formal and overly structured hierarchies, you will be slowing down innovation and response times, (2) departmental silos—this has been discussed (at length) in other sections of this book, but I cannot stress the importance of this enough—having communication blocks between any departments is harmful to the speed and progress of your business, as well as hindering the vast quantities of incredibly useful data flowing between departments, and finally, (3) break down the walls of your organization to the outside world—integration is not only important internally, but also externally. (4) Involve your market in your business, find your business's role in the community and allow your employees to establish a voice—singlehandedly this will drive trust, integration, innovation and loyalty. Four key components of any social business.

Integration is notoriously hard to achieve, and few businesses see the benefit, but if you can demonstrate the value it will have to your business, and the leadership function can give it enough focus and attention, your business will become a social business in a much shorter space of time.

■ **Focus on your business**

■ If your products and services are not delivering the right value to your market, no one will care about your brand.

■ A two-page spread in the Wall Street journal on your business is great, but never forget who pays the bills.

- Focus on fixing your business first, do not rely on a great "brand image" to paper over the cracks. Social technology is like make-up remover.

We have already extensively labored over the switch between the importance of your brand and your business, but this honestly cannot be more important to recognize. In an age of enforced corporate transparency, if your business, or products and services do not deliver what is expected, people are going to complain and discuss this failure with their networks. At this point, redemption becomes a much more difficult task, so focusing on delivering the best possible product or service to the market, and iteratively innovating it, based on insights and feedback is going to prove invaluable to building a business that people trust—promoting your new brand relaunch with matching eloquent story about the founders does not count for anything if the products and services that you deliver are inadequate. However, once you have started to build trust between your business and the market, you then have permission to start talking more widely about your brand—people will want to hear the how, where, why and what of your business—they will actively buy into it, be entertained by it and share it with their friends, but only once you have delivered on your product and service promises. Even if you are the life of the party, if you stand your friends up one too many times, they are not going to care why, because you have damaged your reputation on delivery, and that is the most important aspect of your business; deliver the products and services that people want, then wrap around the beautiful narrative.

Social technology is the business equivalent of make-up remover—if your business is hiding a terrible skin condition, people are going to find out. Be honest about your business and never "spin" or marketing your way toward a lie, because people will find out. Focus your energies instead on fixing the underlying issues, ensuring that your business is as great as it possibly can be, then use the "brand image" as the cosmetic last touches. Do not paper over the cracks in your business.

One of the most common trappings of the successful business is complacency—both internally and externally. It is easy to reach the position of market leader and then feel like you can stop for a breather, but you cannot. This is the most important time in your business's development and every time you stop for a rest, a competitor is gaining on you to steal that market lead.

NEVER STOP

That interview with the chief executive in the national trade magazine is great for promotion among your competitors and the confidence of your shareholders, but unless it is going to have a direct impact on the bottom line, it is almost meaningless. Do everything for a reason, and always make that reason providing better products and services for your market.

Focus on making your business the best it can be and while ever your organization is making things people want and reacting to the market, competitors won't make a dent in your armor.

- Focus on the meaningful
- So few businesses give a true focus to the meaningful—learn what makes a difference to your business, and improve it.
- Avoid vanity. At all costs.
- Your business needs to create meaning for employees and the market—that can only come from understanding what those two groups find is meaningful.

It is far too easy to address the short-term wins in business, but this does not necessarily mean addressing, or understanding the aspects of your business that truly make a difference, or fixing the serious issues. If the leadership function can identify the core components of the business that have a genuine impact on its employees and the market, then it can focus on improving these aspects and paying less attention to detail on the secondary and tertiary aspects that make little meaningful difference. Hiding behind bureaucracy and red-tape is the coward's way out—address the issues, focus on the meaningful.

Learning what makes a difference to your business can be derived from the sum of the total social data across all of the departments we are about to look at—using the totality of that information to gather macro-insights is the fastest way to figuring out how to make serious strides toward becoming a social business.

Businesses that have implemented basic and early-stage social media projects and campaigns often fall into the trap of vanity metrics—looking at the types of data that give the board an immediate endorphin rush, rather than the more long-term view on what effects the bottom line—avoid this type of measurement and analysis at all costs and look to build reliable and robust measurement systems that integrate clearly with the all departments (where appropriate)—this is how your business will start to locate truly meaningful insights into your employees and market. And please, please, any consultant or agency that promises you that 500,000 views of a YouTube video alone will affect the bottom line, thank them for their time and order them a taxi to their next meeting. Social business is about business—know what makes a difference and know what does not.

What is meaningful does not come from anecdotal information from the CEO's wife—it comes from solid social data that can be used to define need states and desires—it has to be based on the market, rather than focus groups or intuition. The market and your employees *are* your business.

Locating the meaning in your business and market also has a dramatic effect on brand trust—if you can demonstrate that you understand what makes a difference (to both employees and the market), then those two key groups will start to trust your business and your vision. They will loyally follow you anywhere, they will tell their networks about the work that you do, and they will defend you in times of crisis. This type of relationship with employees and the market is the nirvana of modern business-building.

If you can implement and adhere to those ten fundamental tenets (all of which are powered by social technology), your business can become a truly social business, and the same social technology that helps to resolve the washing machine disaster by delivering real-time advice on stemming the flow of water can also support the leadership function in directing the business, highlighting new opportunities, enabling growth and improving operational aspects of your organization.

Social technology affects the whole of your business, so treat it that way.

CHAPTER 7

Marketing and Advertising

With such a large shift taking place in consumer behavior and brand structure, the DNA of marketing has been fundamentally altered. Businesses used to rely on agencies to build their brand through huge broadcast programs that reached millions of homes every night, and now, those same advertising campaigns are being fast-forwarded or skipped. How does an industry founded on the medium of broadcast innovate and move itself forward? I believe that it takes the work that it is been doing for decades and makes it media neutral—an idea that works on television will not necessarily work in a digital space, but why limit your idea to a single medium? The primary objective of these campaigns has always been to increase awareness and consideration, ideas should not be built around the medium and no campaign should lead with a script, instead ideas that people talk about should be the core focus, regardless of how they are received by the consumer.

What is most interesting is that there is a new breed of creative and planner moving through the ranks of agencies—people that cannot remember a time without mobiles or access to the Internet—and these people have truly integrated ideas, because they know no different. They create media agnostic ideas that work across all channels and talk to the consumer in a way that they want to be talked to. The idea of focus groups, ethnographic studies and testing has fallen by the wayside and what has moved into that gap is real-time, iterative testing. Testing propositions, creative and ideas live.

CAMPAIGNS VERSUS ALWAYS ON

The economy and the rise of social technology have brought about two major challenges for marketing and advertising.

- Consumers expect to have an ongoing conversation with a business.

- Campaign cycles and on/off media laydowns are going to have to be rethought—advertising has the opportunity to create ideas that people talk about, share and dissect for months, if not years after the advertising spot has aired—just look at VCCP's work with Compare The Market on the Compare The Meerkat campaign for how creative ideas can populate popular culture, and stay there for years.
- There are no definite start and finish points for ideas and conversations—once it is online, the idea takes on a life of its own and the agency and business have a responsibility to engage with how that idea develops and moves into different conversations—this often forces the brand to become more social and look at how the whole business operates in social space, because as the idea moves through different networks, people add further context to it—when Orange, the UK mobile telecommunications carrier launched Orange Wednesdays (a 2 for 1 cinema ticket scheme, on Wednesdays), it launched a Twitter feed to promote the idea, and it got a lot of traction online (it is a great deal, after all), but it also attracted customer service queries from Orange customers, which the business was not in a position to deal with (on Twitter)—preparation is key.
- If a great brand has a great idea and great products, great (and sustained) conversations will follow providing it is executed in the right way and the business is prepared.
- Marketing budgets are being increasingly scrutinized in order to get the maximum return on investment.

As global economies continue to be in a weak position, consumers are putting much more focus on minimizing risk in their purchasing behavior, as such, businesses have to work much harder to acquire and retain customers. This obviously has a knock-on budget and all budgets come under much stronger scrutiny from the Chief Financial Officer (CFO).

There is also the added pressure of many people in businesses believing that activity on social platforms is free and completely measurable—it is neither of these two things. The resource that has to go into engaging with your market online takes man hours, if not agency fees too, and unfortunately there are few business functions that provide perfect measurement of effectiveness. As we discussed in the chapter 2 on embracing convergence, cheap sales tricks and snake oil salesmen in agencies have made our bed, but now we must lie in it.

As a result, we have to do more for less. We have to stretch creative work from 12-week cycles to 52-week cycles, communications planning has to be integrated across multiple platforms, and the effectiveness of our work is under more scrutiny than ever.

So, once again, a combination of the economy and the increasing role of technology in consumers" lives means that another business function has to work harder, be more integrated and have a solid comprehension of the bigger business picture.

INTEGRATED MARKETING

Integration in marketing communications planning can be difficult to achieve, especially when different agencies look after different channels and functions. However, a simple way of approaching integration is by breaking down the different types of media and understanding their roles in the marketing mix and how they overlap with one another, and then producing a comprehensive channel plan for how each individual channel interacts with the other channels in a complimentary, and more importantly, integrated way. By planning in this way, you increase the chance of an idea spreading through different networks, while also providing a cohesive customer journey through the sales funnel; from awareness to engagement to conversion—giving the CFO a little more evidence for their cost/benefit analysis.

While this approach is going to seem simplistic, it is intentionally so in order to force the strategy to sit over multiple types of media and retain the big picture, and by breaking down the different roles for different media, it also allows the business to distribute budgets based on the importance of the role of each media too (again, hopefully pleasing the CFO).

Owned media

Owned media covers anything that the brand has full control over—so the website, or blog, would be classed as owned media, because the business controls the content that is published there, as well as moderating any conversations that occur on the media.

Owned media also covers most traditional advertising and marketing functions, such as television advertising, direct marketing and on-pack promotions.

Owned media can be a powerful way to stimulate conversations by publishing interesting content and sign-posting other types of media—it is also a great place to drive people to eCommerce, use cookies to track behavior and serve up advertising at a later date, as well as capture data.

The challenge, however, with owned media is that it is likely that your website or blog is not currently the hub of your communities" conversations, which are more likely to be taking place on earned media space—it can be incredibly difficult to try and migrate a community away from where it is comfortable, so that you can host the conversation. Built it and they will come over, thanks to social technology.

Earned media

Earned media is any space where the brand has little control over the conversation other than what it publishes itself in that space. Places like forums, Facebook, Twitter, and blogs are classed as earned media, as the business has to earn the right to be discussed in these places, and has little control over the conversations taking place other than what it publishes itself. Earned media is a great way to drive people into owned spaces—hopefully showcasing the great content that your brand has to offer the community.

There is also obvious cross-over between earned media and owned media, as a brand effectively "owns" its Twitter profile, yet to stimulate conversations in that space it has to "earn" them through conversations that it has little control over.

The downside to earned media is that when used on its own, you have very little control over who can speak to you—the intended content and conversations a brand wants to have are likely to be different from how they are received—intention versus reception is a difficult challenge in earned media.

Paid media

Paid media is self-explanatory—paid media is bought media in spaces that sell advertising space, or sponsored blog posts/advertorials.

This could be in the form of banner advertising, sponsored links in search engine results or promotional content in a magazine. This type of media makes for a great way to target certain audiences online (by smart media buying, and testing), and the paid media can then be used to drive people into owned and earned media. The major challenge with paid media is trust in it has fallen, and the industry average conversion rates of banner advertising and PPC is incredibly low—which means that the media buyer has to work incredibly hard to drive the right people through paid media.

Once you have started to plan which type of media is going to be used for what function, you can begin to build a channel plan. A channel plan is a lot like an electronics schematic—it shows which components are connected to each other, and how the electricity (or conversations, in this case) move between different components (social platforms).

The key to successful channel planning is matching the content you are planning to publish to the right platform, and ensuring that there is a clear call to action from one platform to the next, with mutual links between those platforms where it is appropriate (for example a linked video from a business's YouTube page may push people toward the business's website, but the website may also embed video content from the YouTube channel on its blog—these are the types of consumer journeys that need to be planned properly if you are to keep the attention of the consumer).

Now this is where it starts to get a little more complicated. To ensure your marketing communications is as focused as possible on delivering business results, try and plot your channel plan over the sales funnel. There are two benefits to doing this; the first is that it becomes easy to trim down on unnecessary components of your plan, and the second aspect is that it then allows you to build a KPI framework around each of the three different stages of the funnel.

(A quick caveat: while most sales funnels have four phases (usually *awareness*, *interest*, *desire* and *action*), I am a firm believer that there is a lot of crossover between *awareness* and *interest*, and *interest* and *desire*, so I usually use three phases instead.)

AWARENESS

- How do you plan to stimulate awareness around your content or creative?

- How do you plan on staggering content or creative so that the awareness phase acts as a taster for consumers and provides a clear call to action to click into the next phase of the funnel?
- Which elements of owned, earned and paid media can act as attention grabbers in visible spaces? The types of components to consider (among a myriad of others) are
  - ☐ Banner advertising on popular forums
  - ☐ Blogger relations to secure editorial coverage on influential blogs
  - ☐ YouTube video content introducing the content or creative
  - ☐ On-pack promotions
- How do you plan on tracking traffic into the next phase of the funnel?

ENGAGEMENT

- Once you have captured the attention of your audience and they are into the next phase of the funnel, what are you going to offer them to stimulate conversations?
- Where do you plan to engage with the consumer? Is it a Facebook page for your business? Or could it be over email? How do you plan to amplify the engagement that will hopefully take place to raise awareness?
- How are you going to encourage people to share content with their networks?
- Do you have a calendar for ongoing engagement?

CONVERSION

- If it is possible, how do you plan to incentivize the conversion?
- Which data would you suggest is captured?
- What is the next phase of engagement?
- Where does this conversion take place? It could be through Facebook, or your own eCommerce site—it might even be a third-party retailer.

Once you have started to think about marketing communications in this way, it provides real structure and focus to your strategy—through clear objectives and a cohesive user journey from awareness to conversion.

THE EMOTIONAL VERSUS THE RATIONAL

People use social platforms for a variety of different reasons; from keeping up with old friends to finding new music—the social web is what you want to make of it, and there is a community for literally everyone. The motivations for people using certain social platforms usually fit into one of two categories, based on the content, network and usage of the platform. Those two categories are *emotional* and *rational*.

Emotional spaces

The term emotional space does not necessarily correspondent to a *state of emotion*, more so the mindset of the person while they are using that social technology. For instance, Facebook is often used as an emotional space, because people are looking to speak to friends, share updates about their life, and more often than not, people are looking to be entertained, rather than sold to. This usually indicates that emotional spaces are great for business to tell the story of their brand and provide brand-based content that is not focused on the hard sell. A great example of this is the Tippex YouTube takeover that launched in 2011—a simple concept using interactive video and simple creative, users could choose different words and the video content would display different scenarios. While this inevitably increased awareness, it was an idea that played purely to the emotional, entertainment space, rather than driving a rational purchasing decision.

Rational spaces

Rational spaces refer to the types of places that people visit online to ask questions and seek advice from peers (not necessarily friends). These are spaces like forums and blogs were content is often lead by opinion and insight, rather than lifestreaming (as is more common in emotional spaces), and these spaces are usually lead by the interest graph, rather than the social graph. These are great spaces for businesses to occupy in terms of providing straight forward content, advice and demonstrating product benefits. Usually people are in the frame of mind to make a purchase, so this is the perfect time for a business to avoid brand storytelling and focus on providing information and support. A fantastic case study to look at for this type of activity is BestBuy's Twelpforce, where sales staff where given access to Twitter at work and encouraged to help people asking questions on the microblogging platform—the team currently responds to around 150 questions *every day*.

There are obvious outliers to this theory, businesses that manage to find a careful balance between emotional and rational spaces and capture the attention of consumers at the perfect time. Businesses such as BlendTec is an incredible example of a business that managed to create entertaining content that had the rational product benefits at the core of the idea—the Will It Blend video series on YouTube has had nearly 200 million combined video views across its channel.

While BlendTec is a great example of a business that has made a huge impact by combining emotional and rational content, most businesses cannot achieve the same result, and this is down to the nature of their business. Understanding your business's role in these two very different spaces takes time and research, but it can be massively fruitful and helps shape the your business and brand marketing communications, giving your content the maximum opportunity to raise awareness, drive engagement and ultimately drive conversions.

Now we have covered off integrated marketing communications using social technology, let us look at how you can incorporate different aspects of social technology into the various marketing disciplines.

PLANNING

The planning function of any marketing agency usually bases all of its strategy and planning on insights—these are traditionally derived from ethnographical studies, research groups and quantitative research, but now with the new raft of Big Data available, planners and strategists have a new arsenal of insights to draw from when building a case for their work. Most planners will work from three types of insight; the market, the product/brand and the audience, and social research can add to all three of these—with usually more robust and reliable data than traditional research methods. I have picked apart some of the potential applications of research using social technology below.

■ The market (understanding what the competitor landscape looks like)

- What are people saying about your competitors online?
- What is the share of voice between your competitors? Does this match with market share? If not, why might it not?
- What sort of social activity do your competitors carry out in social spaces?
- What is the context of conversations around your competitors?
- What is the sentiment around the mentions of your competitors?
- Where do these conversations take place?
- What do your competitors' reputations look like through search engine results?
- What type of search terms are people using to search for your competitors with?
- Has there been any spike in search engine queries over the last 12 months for your competitors? If so, why?
- Are there any examples of best practice within the competitor landscape?
- The product/brand
  - ☐ What is the existing volume of conversation around the product/brand?
  - ☐ Where do these conversations take place?
  - ☐ What is the sentiment of these conversations?
  - ☐ What is the context of these conversations?
  - ☐ Within the competitor landscape, what is your business's share of voice?
  - ☐ What does your business's reputation look like through search engine results?
  - ☐ Has there been any spike in search engine queries for your brand over the last 12 months? If so, why?
  - ☐ What existing activity is your business carrying out in social spaces? Is it successful?
- The audience
  - ☐ What is the size of the volume of conversations around this category?
  - ☐ Which social platforms does this audience use the most?
  - ☐ What is their typical behavior online?
  - ☐ What content/messaging are they receptive to?
  - ☐ What sort of terms does this audience search for in relation to the category?
  - ☐ Who are the influential voices in your category?

This list is far from exhaustive, but gives a pretty accurate depiction of the types of insights that planners and strategists can gather from social data when working with your business.

CREATIVE

The creative's role is to turn insights and strategy into an idea that taps into social and cultural consciousness—which makes the social web an invaluable resource for finding grassroots cultural phenomena that can be used as inspiration, or added to by the business to create something of social and cultural worth that translates well into existing behavior and interests. These types of phenomena are often called "memes," and are micro-trends that circulate at rapid speed through networks of friends—either by email, text or social communication. A few years ago there was a series of adverts for a milkshake brand called Crusha that featured images of animals that had been animated in a lo-fi way, singing the Crusha theme tune—this idea was originally born online years earlier and took off at incredible speed. The creative used in the advert ran for more than three years and had incredible cultural currency.

The social web also opens up a number of new routes for creatives; from the bespoke video response work of the Isaiah Mustafa in Old Spice Guy adverts, to GAP crowd-sourcing the redesign of its ill-fated new logo through social platforms. As mentioned in previous chapters, the new breed of creatives rising through the ranks of agencies are creating ideas that are media agnostic—they create ideas that people talk about, regardless of where they have seen them.

There is also a big opportunity for creatives to test new creative propositions using social technology too. Simple mechanisms like closed Facebook Groups, or password-protected forums allow creatives to invite core customers and influencers within the category to review new propositions, giving honest feedback, but in an environment that ensures the new creative work is kept away from the masses while it is still being developed.

MEDIA BUYING

While the role that social technology can play in media buying is not immediately apparent, in my opinion, it has the potential to be one of the strongest uses across the marketing mix. In its most simple incarnation, media buying is about purchasing media for advertising and marketing creative that is seen by the right target audience, at the right time.

There is also a massive opportunity to combine media buying with social media outreach and influencer engagement—this can be seen as a multifaceted approach to driving awareness, engagement, *and* conversion. By sharing knowledge between the two disciplines and creating an integrated strategy we can target earned and paid spaces with both rational and emotional messaging—creating a two-pronged approach to building trust and influence from an emotional perspective, while also serving rational, product-driven advertising in paid media in the same space. Let us look at an example: a breakdown recovery service is looking for people in need expressing issues in social spaces where it can offer advice and guidance, the team finds a forum thread filled with people having a similar issue, so the team replies to the thread offering advice and a comprehensive solution to the problems people are experiencing. Meanwhile, the media department has been notified that this engagement is taking place, so that it can then approach the forum owner about purchasing media space alongside the very same forum thread—by solving the problems and providing valuable advice the business is positioning itself as a reliable expert, while displayed next to the forum thread is a direct response banner advertisement offering discount breakdown cover *from the same business*. The customer journey writes itself on this one.

Media agencies are already experienced in using agile and A/B testing and digital advertising, but there is also another opportunity for testing this type of paid media—using information from the owned and earned space to analyze consumer behavior and tastes to help shape the creative being used in the digital display adverts. By combining these two sets of data, you can begin to build a really accurate picture of how communities behave online in relation to paid media—micro-testing, tweaking creative slightly and allowing the brand to focus all of its resources on advertising that drives conversions.

THE WEBSITE

For many businesses, the humble website is their first foray into the online world, we have seen websites take the transition from the

1990s "brouchure-ware" websites, to eCommerce, to micro-sites, and now, finally, forward thinking businesses have begun to build socially integrated business and brand hubs. The importance of this social integration cannot be underestimated, simple tweaks to existing technology can allow consumers to log in to your website through Facebook, or Twitter, at which point you can personalize their whole experience, based on their social data (Netflix is a great example of this when it delivers messaging such as "Your friend Peter recently watched *Arrested Development*"—powerful personalization and peer recommendation). It goes much deeper than that though, using that social data, your business can begin to build stronger profiles of people visiting your website—from their behavior on the site to their social graph—but you must provide something in return for this, this is a value exchange that most savvy online consumers understand, "I'm giving you my data, in return for what?" If you offer something of value, then you can begin to pair social data with existing digital analytics and A/B testing to drive really powerful user behavior insights—all of which can then be fed back into the organization and be delivered to the Chief Data Officer.

Your website can also be used to add a lot of context to your business and enhance perceptions of expertise and understanding—simple additions such as a blog will allow your employees to showcase their knowledge of the category that your business operates in, and by encouraging your businesses bloggers to engage in the community, you can start to improve the influence of your employees and awareness of your brands knowledge. If it is done in the right way, your website can become part of the community that is your market—for evidence of this, look at businesses like Cisco or IBM, both of which have developed extensive online influence and community involvement through allowing employees to publish blog posts on their main business website.

The final aspect that I believe that no businesses website should be without is a newsroom and media library. Not only for journalists and the media but for anyone looking for information about your business—from simple boiler plates to video interviews with key staff, this type of content can add a lot of value to people's perceptions of what your business stands for. In the next chapter, I will also explore the role that digital newsrooms can play in a crisis communications situation.

SEARCH ENGINE OPTIMIZATION

Search engine optimization is the older brother of social technology, with search engines preceding social technology by at least ten years, but there is a natural kinship between the two because of the way that search engines use social media in their search results. Google announced in 2010 that it was going to start giving preference to social media content in search results, as well as (when possible) displaying YouTube content on the first page (remember that Google owns YouTube) and this has had a massive impact on the way that search engine optimization teams work, with many now carrying out blogger and influencer outreach as well as paid search activities too.

So social technology obviously plays a huge role in search engine optimization—but there are additional ways in which search specialists can use data from social technologies. When news and trends break online, the first place that they tend to break is on Twitter (and in the Chapter 4, I outlined how you can use this data)—now if your business wants to be truly agile and they have value to add to news or an emerging trend, one way to reach people is by buying pay-per-click (PPC) advertising on emerging terms— we know that there is a correlation between emerging trends on rapid platforms like Twitter and increases in keyword search volumes through Google—so if you can spot the trend, you can place the reactive PPC advertisement.

From an organic search point of view, there is a lot of crossover between the public relations, marketing and search functions in terms of content creation—public relations seeds content with influencers, marketing produces content to distribute online and search produces content to impact on organic search—and in the majority of cases, this content is not shared between the different departments. However, if your business is to embrace this open culture, the first step is getting departments that have obvious cross over to talk to each other and share departmental strategies— eradicating all-too-common situations like this.

IN-STORE MARKETING

Just because a consumer is in an offline store, does not mean that there is not a role for social technology. When consumers are in a retail environment, sales and marketing staff have additional time to build relationships with consumers and make them aware of the digital aspects of the business.

Simple proximity and location promotions are a great place to start—you only have to look at the volume of bars and coffee shops that give away free products to the FourSquare Mayor of their retail store to realize the potential power of location-based social media marketing—in simple terms, to retain their Mayorship, people have to "check-in" to your store every time they are there, and every time they do this it alerts all of their network to their location. While FourSquare and Facebook Places may increase the chances of serendipitous meetings, from the perspective of a business, it also generates peer review. If one of your close friends is repeatedly checking-in to a certain store or bar, it is going to pique your interest—at which point you are more likely to visit the store or bar to see why your friend spends so much time there, or at least talk to them about the store or bar.

As with almost all of the marketing disciplines, it is important to focus on providing a value exchange in return for this word of mouth and social data, but the potential rewards are high.

MOBILE

Along with experiential, mobile is one of the most exciting aspects of marketing (even though mobile can cross multiple business boundaries—from internal communications to customer retention) because it helps to demonstrate the converged world. More people have a mobile phone now than people have access to clean water; as depressing as this statistic is, it tells us that mobile is an incredibly powerful platform that cannot be ignored by businesses. There are numerous aspects of social technology that can help improve the mobile experience for people using the application or site—simple things like enabling people to sign in to the application using their social platform details (Twitter or Facebook are the most popular ways to do this), and allowing people to share content directly from the application with their social graphs.

There are a few important lessons that we can learn from social platforms when it comes to mobile though.

- Your mobile application must add value and not become a me-too application—80 percent of iPhone applications are used a single time and never used again, with branded applications suffering from this in particular.

- Mobile is about here and now, and businesses should respect that—do not expect to build an attention-demanding application that is full of sales promotion material and see usage beyond the first 15 seconds.

Mobile should be an always on, hygiene factor that every brand understands—with more than 4 billion people with mobiles, and that technology increasing day by day, mobile is no longer a luxury—it is a necessity. And think beyond Apple, in fact think beyond the handheld device—think about tablets, think about people without smartphones. Your mobile strategy should not really be a mobile strategy, it should be a mobility strategy—how your business can improve and enhance consumers' experiences' beyond the desktop computer, through technology.

EXPERIENTIAL

Marketing campaigns that involve outdoor activity and events have always been fun to be involved in for the people actually attending the event, but with social technology we can now throw these events open to the world (or a select number of influencers, depending on the objectives of the event!). There are three elements of experiential activity that I feel social technology can add value to.

Live-streaming

Broadcasting your event live onto a social platform such as YouTube or Vimeo has been extremely popular with technology businesses that have been launching new products or services simultaneously in multiple countries over the few years—the actual event itself may only have a few key media from the host country in actual attendance, but because the event is live-streamed there is the opportunity for tens of thousands of influential voices to witness the event. Some technology businesses even go as far to send full press packs to people watching the live-stream from home so that they feel like they are at the actual event. Of course, sometimes you would like your event to be kept to a select number of people—for which you can provide login details to a protected live-stream—reaching the right people across the world, but not exposing anything that is still to be launched to a mass audience.

The best example of a business using this type of technology, for me, comes from the premium Vodka brand Smirnoff. In 2011 Smirnoff launched The Smirnoff Nightlife Exchange Project. The premise of the project was simple, but executed fantastically well. Smirnoff wanted to give the best nightlife experiences from around the world to people in different cities, so in addition to recreating different cultural nightlives in different cities (Miami came to London, Italy went to Australia)—it would also live-stream the whole event, one city after another, allowing anyone around the world to witness the event and experience the idea.

Widening out invitations to online influencers

It is now widely accepted that many online writers carry as much, if not more, influence than many of traditional journalists. From Gawker to ShinyShiny, many of these online organizations' readerships eclipse those of many of the UK's national newspapers. With this in mind, bloggers are increasingly being invited as key media to brand and business events—from roundtable discussions with the CEO of a business to London Fashion Week, online influencers are everywhere, and they are writing about it prolifically too, but not just for their magazine, also for the personal networks, using services like Instagram, Twitter and Vimeo to document their experiences, to be shared with millions of people online. If you are not inviting online influencers to your events, you are missing out on a huge opportunity.

Random acts of kindness

Experiential marketing activities are not only limited to events, and a rising trend over the last few years has been using social data to provide people with random acts of kindness. The simplest use of RAK is for a business to use social data to find someone (either a customer or not) who is having a bad day, or who deserves rewarding (for whatever reason)—the business then delivers that reward, out of the blue. One of the best examples of this type of activity was from Stella, when it launched its new cider brand, Cidre, in the UK. The marketing team located influential FourSquare mayors across the city of London and delivered crates of Cidre to them—however, the delivery was not just any old DHL delivery, the character from the television advertising hand delivered the crates in full costume and character. This is powerful marketing that merges online and offline, and generates a huge volume of word of mouth. Great work from Stella.

CONCLUSION

One of the core tenets to this book is the convergence between the offline and online worlds, and in few places is it best demonstrated than experiential marketing. From Instagram photography competitions, to live-streaming of product launches, experiential marketing is in a great place to demonstrate the power of our new, converged world.

The way in which we market our business, products and services has not changed fundamentally, but the additional access that we have to data through social technology has started to alter the way in which we view marketing. Remember Mr. Wanamaker's quote about advertising? "Half the money I spend on advertising is wasted; the trouble is I don't know which half." Social data means that we can minimize the wasted money, we can narrow down on our target audience, we can test propositions and creative before we launch it into a mass market, and we can *involve more people* in what we do.

As you can see from this chapter, there are few disciplines within marketing that are not going to see a positive impact from your business becoming social—everything else aside, having each department talking to each other more frequently will make a massive impact. The idea of integration within marketing has been a hot topic for years, coming in and going out of business fashion, but regardless of fashion, it is important that each discipline understands what the wider department is doing—without this, all effort is going to be counter-intuitive to achieving core business objectives.

There are five fundamental rules that the marketing department in a social business should follow:

1. **Put integration at the heart of every strategy**
   Consumers do not see the departments of your business, they do not view your brand as a series of different teams, rather they see a whole brand, and your marketing has to overcome the complexity of organizational structure and communications to present a single brand. Integrating owned, earned, and paid media will help to present this notion of a single brand entity, enhance the consumer journey from awareness, engagement and on to conversion, and ultimately give your brand a much stronger chance of making sales using social platforms.

2. **Understand how to use social data**
   The role of social data in business is massive, it is a factor in every chapter in this book and for strategy and marketing communication planning it is equally as important, if not more important. Understanding the possibilities (and limitations) of what sort and scale of data that can be gathered from social technology is going to seriously bolster business, brand, competitor, and audience insights in a way that your planning department has never seen before. Raw, unadulterated data, direct from your market.

3. **Stay close to your audience**
   One of the fundamental reasons for your business becoming a social business is that it can be more reactive and agile to consumers; if your marketing department can do this too, it sends out a strong signal to your customers, competitors, and employees that your business is listening to the market, and reacting accordingly.

4. **Use social technology to widen participation in your business**
   Every business has internal experts, people with decades of experience of working within the industry, people who know your business's products and services inside out, but these people exist outside of your business too, and if you can involve them and make them feel part of the fabric of your business, they can become very powerful advocates.

5. **Talk about your products and your brand story at the right time**

   It is arrogant to think that social media is just about businesses selling products. It is not. It is, however, about old friends connecting, about learning new information, about seeing the far reaches of the globe from your lounge. Your marketing department needs to take time to learn about your market, their behavior and how they use certain social platforms so that it can convey the right type of message at the right time.

Follow these five rules and your marketing department should see some short-term wins, live by these rules and your marketing department will help your whole business to become more social.

CHAPTER 8

Public Relations

Public relations departments and agencies were, arguably, the first business department to really "get" social media—with early work from the likes of Edelman and Marriott Hotels taking place in 2004/2005. One of the reasons I think this happened is that public relations practitioners focus on two things;

- Creating ideas that get people talking (such as press stunts and crafting stories from dry statistics).
- Shaping public opinion.

Now, in my opinion (in the old world), these two things fit perfectly with social media. Good ideas are shared quickly between people because technology enables fast sharing (the KONY video hit 120 million views in less than 48 hours) and public relations practitioners have direct access to the people that they are trying to reach through the traditional media. However, this has been massively abused over the last five years; from astroturfing to reputation band-aids on Wikipedia and mass email mailouts to bloggers. Social media quickly became used as a "quick fix" with tangible (but empty) metrics that could be reported back to the brand.

However, I believe that there is a huge opportunity for those with public relations skills to work alongside other disciplines to create ideas for businesses and brands that are based on things that people are interested in—traditionally public relations is a sink or swim industry for creative ideas, either the journalist likes the idea or they do not, so public relations practitioners have to understand their audience inherently, crafting an approach that is almost guaranteed to capture the interest of the journalist. This approach lends itself incredibly well to this new world; understanding the audience, crafting ideas that people are going to be interested in; this is the sort of collaborative, research driven approach that fits in the new world.

One of the great modern public relations practitioners (and my mentor), the late Mark Hanson, drew a diagram for me early in my career, he drew it on the back of scrap paper that I still carry with me to this day, it was a simple diagram, but explained the shift that the public relations industry has gone through over the last 15 years perfectly.

Since the early 1900s, public relations practitioners have gone through the following process to influence the public (Figure 5).

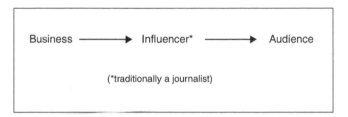

Figure 5   A traditional communications flow

Yet with the increasing accessibility of technology giving everyone and anyone a voice, this process has changed (Figure 6).

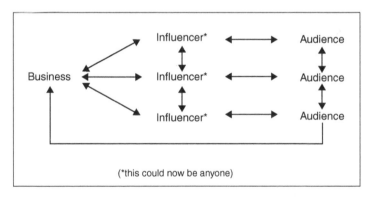

Figure 6   A modernised communications flow

It is a simple diagram, but yet so many public relations professionals fail to grasp that the concept of who is "the media" has changed. Public relations has undergone a huge shift over the last five years as businesses have started to finally broaden out their definition of who constitutes to an influencer—with launch events now flooded with a mixture of the mainstream media and niche bloggers. This is for the reasons highlighted in Figure 6: (1) the mainstream media has started to use social media increasingly to research stories and features, often finding content on niche blogs and forums and building on that information to build stories, (2) bloggers are often involved in high-profile leaks on new product launches, usually because they have direct access to someone within the business and few respect corporate secrecy (why should they?), and finally (3) online media have a massive influence online, not just through readership, but also through search—search playing a huge role in the customer journey.

There is, however, a major challenge. In general, public relations does not currently have a seat at board level and the agency is often briefed on work after the advertising or media agency has produced the idea, so being so far downstream from where the strategic decisions are made makes it difficult for public relations people to have the impact they deserve. I speak from experience, as my career started in public relations and one thing that I can confidently say having moved into the advertising industry is that the different marketing disciplines need people with public relations experience to work alongside existing teams to ensure that ideas are going to stimulate conversations, that they will be talked about in bars and that people will sustain interest in them after the media lay down has finished.

What follows is a breakdown of how social technology can be used across different parts of the public relations function, exploring the changing role of the public relations practitioner and how social technology is having an impact on the everyday role of the public relations professional.

MODERN MEDIA RELATIONS

Over the last 20 years the role of the journalist has fundamentally changed—from the way in which news is reported, to the volume of work expected to be produced—and technology has played a major role in this. The workload has increased, the headcount has fallen, and journalists working in today's newsrooms are expected to include different media in their work, so that articles can be published immediately online. This increase in pressure has been paralleled by a rise in "citizen journalists"—everyday people armed with an Internet connection and an opinion.

Many people over the last five years have called time on media relations, declaring that "citizen journalism" has overtaken the role of the traditional journalist—now, in my opinion, this is looking at media relations and the influence that the media hold the wrong way. The way in which news breaks *has* fundamentally changed, we just have to look at the way in which the Egyptian riots were reported in 2011 (with an almost complete media blackout in Egypt and a ban on foreign media reporting from the scene of the riots, the only way in which we knew that it was happening was through citizens capturing videos and uploading them to YouTube and people using proxies to access Twitter and distribute short messages about what was happening). However, I would argue that the role of the professional journalist (those that are trained, regulated and balanced in their opinions) still hold a core position in society and have a responsibility to add context to news, to explore the different aspects of stories and to add information that citizen journalists may not possess to provide the full story. In our role as consumers of news, we need to be presented with the facts, and in far too many cases citizen journalists report from an incredibly biased position—they are not held to account, so how can the public relations function of a social business work with a modern journalist? As it always has, it comes down to understanding the needs and pressures of the journalist you are interested in talking to.

It is not only businesses that have seen the impact of Big Data, the way in which journalists source stories has also changed—with data from social and digital sources now playing a major role in the news agenda. From tweets being read out on the evening news, to journalists using search trends to predict potential high traffic stories for the newspapers website—social data has flooded into the newsrooms, so much so many national newspaper newsrooms now display their own online data above the news desks. So, how can the public relations function of your business adapt to this modern media landscape?

Well, gone are the days when a press release in an email with a photograph attached would suffice, with journalists now expected to provide multiple media types (videos, numerous photos for galleries, live chats with spokespeople, links to social platforms, infographics, data, the list goes on) it is incredibly important for the public relations department to "package" news in a different way.

The art of public relations is now finding itself surrounded by people in lab coats with spreadsheets.

Working with the media has always involved understanding the journalist and know what they are interested in writing about, so your public relations team now has to start using the same techniques that modern journalists do to find stories—watching for breaking trends, using RSS feeds from "feeder sources" (the sources that influence the media, such as the Guido Fawkes blog), and analyzing search behaviors to see what sort of topics are picking up steam. All of this allows the public relations department to spot the same stories that the media are spotting, and then quickly analyze where your business might be able to add value.

One of the other major benefits that social technology has brought into the public relations department is the ability to forge stronger relationships with journalists and connect with them more frequently and less formally. When I started my first role in marketing, it was in a public relations department, and I joined just as Twitter launched. Intrigued by hearing people talk about the service, I joined and started to "follow" a few journalists that I read regularly, and a few that I thought would be interesting from a professional perspective. Before long I was talking regularly with national newspaper journalists about everything from music that we had a shared interest in (electronica, if you would like to know) to what was in the news that day. This type of regular contact helps you to build relationships quickly with journalists and understand what makes them tick—I was six months into my first job and my contacts list contained dozens of journalists from each of the UK's national media!

In today's modernized media landscape, there are two things that are important; packaging up your news story as comprehensively as possible with as much detail and media as you can, and using Big Data to understand what sort of stories might be hitting the news agenda soon.

BLOGGER RELATIONS

So, as previously mentioned, alongside the changing role of journalists through technology, we have also seen the rise of influencers online, building audiences, writing regularly, and breaking big news stories. These people are bloggers. What started as a term to depict an online journal (which is why posts are mostly stored chronologically) has become a new form of media outlet—from Gawker and CNET to niche music blogs and photoblogs, bloggers are becoming media stars in their own right. One of the world's most visited blogs, The Huffington Post, was bought by AOL in 2011 and regularly exceeds 30 million unique readers a month—making it and thousands of other blogs incredibly influential (and this is without taking into account the effect that they have on search engine results). So, how does your business engage with this new type of media?

Well, blogger relations has many similarities to media relations—you need to understand the author, what interests them, what they are likely to write about, and what value the information about your business or products can add to their post. There are hundreds of examples of blogger relations done well, as well as done very badly; for best practice, see the Marmarati campaign that the agency We Are Social carried out in 2009.

I have been involved in more than 50 blogger relations projects over the last six years, and hopefully some of the things that I have got right (and got wrong) can help your public relations department to successfully engage with bloggers. However, a brief caveat, bloggers are *not* regulated media and reactions to a business attempting to engage with a blogger can vary, depending on lots of different factors.

Blogger relations: A simple guide

- Identify the role that you feel blogger relations should play in your overall marketing and public relations strategy—is your objective to raise awareness by generating a large volume of coverage, or is your objective to select a few choice influencers to seed stories with that you know will then spread to offline media? Clearly defined objectives are the bedrock of any successful strategy.
- Identify the bloggers that you think will be interested in the content that you have—this can be done through simple Google searches around the category that your business operates in, or through a more sophisticated social media tool such as BrandWatch.
- Research each blogger **thoroughly**. Just because they have published content before, does not mean that they are going to

publish the same sort of content again. You need to understand how they write, what they care about, if they are receptive to engagement from businesses and what they are like personally.

- Craft individual emails to each blogger—none of this "Dear Bloggers" activity, as that is sure to get your email deleted.
- Speak to the blogger in a professional, yet informal tone—give up some details about yourself, *build a relationship*.

In addition to the guide above, there are a few basic rules that will help your public relations department avoid run-ins with bloggers.

- Always research the blogger that you are planning on speaking to.
- Explain who you are, where you work, and why you are getting in touch up front—do not hide it at the end of the email.
- Never treat a blogger like a second-class media citizen—they are likely to have a much bigger influence on your market than you think.
- Never mass mail bloggers, or mail merge, or copy and paste emails—bloggers talk to each other, and they will find out and then laugh at you (and probably publicly).
- Avoid attachments like the plague.
- Like in media relations, encapsulate the whole email in the first few sentences—influential bloggers get between 100 and 500 emails *everyday.*

Blogger relations can be incredibly beneficial to your business; from the point of view of building a relationship with someone influential, to reaching a large audience that is your target market, to blog posts appearing search engine results when your market Googles you. If you get blogger relations right, it can produce a fruitful and meaningful relationship for the long term.

UNDERSTANDING NEWS FLOW ONLINE

Once your public relations department has become a little more comfortable engaging with online influencers, we can start to apply a little bit more science to the art. News travels incredibly quickly online, through a combination of relationships between bloggers, RSS readers, Twitter and links between blogs, news can spread in a matter of minutes. The effect that this hyper-connectivity has on business can be both beneficial (when you have good news that is interesting) and harmful (say a product leak, or a crisis situation), so gaining a better understanding of how news travels through your online community can be incredibly useful.

As mentioned in previous chapters, understanding networks is absolutely key for a social business. We have previously looked at how information moves in, around, and outside of your business, but how does information move around between the influencers in your industry? The same principles apply—if you can track and analyze the social data that surrounds the network, you can begin to form a much more comprehensive understanding of how the dynamics work, giving a much clearer indication of where new information usually comes from, how it spreads, how it reaches critical mass, and how it then spreads across the whole network.

At my previous agency, I used to work with a technology company that often suffered from product leaks early on in the research and development stage that made announcements and launches stunted in nature, because most people already knew all of the details before the product had actually been finalized and launched, so I developed a simple system for tracking how news spread across the web using a combination of freely available social data, manual analysis and my relationships with the community. The system was basic, but helped to both visualize and understand how information passed from one blogger to another, and it (usually) helped identify where the information originated. The system was far from perfect, but after running a series of sample tests, it became quite useful. Outlined below is the process that I developed to track the spread of information across online media.

- Identify a unique keyword that would most certainly feature in all blog posts (or at least series of keywords that are in direct relation to the story)—in my experience, this was a new product name.
- Use Google to collect all of the content that has been published with this keyword in, across a certain timeframe (this is based on how long ago the story broke).
- Use a free data scraping tool to pull all of the search results into a spreadsheet—the data scraper should be calibrated to create a separate field for the "date published" data.

- Sort the spreadsheet by the "date published" field—this should reveal the original source, however it is important to manually check this by checking the content to see if there are any other sources attributed to the post.
- Then, using a simple script that a programmer can easily create, you need to analyze each of the blogs for outbound links— creating another spreadsheet that lists which of the blogs that covered the news story link to each other, and which other blogs (that did not publish content on the story) they link to as well.
- You can then use a free program like Gephi to turn this spreadsheet into a network graph and see exactly how the news spread from one blog to another, and where it is likely to spread to next.

Once you have run this as a trial across a sample of four or five stories, you can begin to build a feasibly accurate picture of how news spreads within you industry, and how regularly starts the spread of news, which is massively useful in terms of controlling links and finding influential people to start to build relationships with.

INVESTOR RELATIONS

Investor relations can be difficult to maintain unless your business is a huge corporation, but social technology enables your business to distribute key information about the organization regularly and informally (in co-ordination with the more formal aspects of investor relations). However, the most interesting aspect of maintaining a dialogue with investors through social technology is the level of additional information and context that you can provide.

From live-streaming of investor conferences through social technology, to daily updates on business performance through a closed social network, you can bring your business's benefactors closer into the organization and make them feel like they have much more visibility (if they choose so) on how the business operates. There is also the opportunity to use social technology to source ideas from investors, who may want much more hands on involvement in the direction of the business, by setting up weekly surgeries with investors (either on a one to one basis, or as a group).

The most important thing is to understand how involved your investors want to be, and what the most convenient method of communication is with which to speak to them, but the opportunity to help investors feel closer to the business should be exciting for any social business.

MAKING INFORMATION PUBLIC

Once your public relations team has started engaging with bloggers, your team is going to find an increasing number of requests for information coming into the department, a simple way to deal with this is to create a section on the website that houses a library of content that people can access, and that appears in search results when people Google your brand. This reduces the amount of time that the department has to spend sourcing images, shooting videos and finding out information about the business to then distribute to people interested in the company (and potentially interested in writing about the business and its products).

Your public relations department may already have a library of content stored offline, for journalist enquiries, or even a newsroom hosted on the website, but the important part of having this information is allowing people to freely access it, including the public.

SPIN, TRANSPARENCY AND WIKIPEDIA

Public relations professionals have, for a long time now, had a reputation of "spinning" the truth and hiding negative aspects of news to help avoid them being aired publicly, this is partly down to the history of the industry, partly down to politics, and partly down to the industry having a dark side where a few unscrupulous agencies lurk in the shadows. However, the rise in social platforms has also seen an increase in whistleblowers and the audience for their content—making spin a dangerous prospect for any business— especially when your own employees could be potentially leaking information on social platforms (either intentionally, or unintentionally). In my opinion, spin and the "massaging" of news indicates that there are more important issues that need to be addressed inside your business before you can become a social, open business.

"Openness" is about transparency, breaking down the walls of your business and inviting people in, even the media. The age of corporate secrecy is over, just check Wikileaks and see for yourself. This, however, is a good thing, and this type of radical transparency should be embraced—if you have cleaned out your corporate closet, so to speak, then people (whether they are media, online influencers or employees) are not going to find anything worth blowing the whistle on.

As a side note, and before I move on using social technology to help support reputation management, I would like to quickly talk about Wikipedia, as many businesses still see the site as an opportunity to "shape" perceptions of their organization. While Wikipedia is incredibly visible (when there is a Wikipedia entry for the search term you have just typed into Google, Wikipedia is usually in the top four results) and people around the world (rightly or wrongly) use it as a source for accurate and unbiased information; you must realize that Wikipedia is a community-driven project, with thousands of editors and hundreds of thousands of contributors all over the world working together to provide accurate information on all many of subjects—it is not a place for corporate speak, spin or squabbles. Your public relations department should definitely have an eye on the site, but they must not create entries on behalf of your business, edit pages under pseudonyms, or try to mislead people by removing or editing certain sections of entries. The one thing that they must absolutely do is read the rules and regulations for the site—there have been countless stories in the media of businesses being caught breaking the rules and then publicly ousted for their troubles—if you have an issue with the content on a Wikipedia page that relates to your business or products, contact an editor and discuss it with them directly.

REPUTATION MANAGEMENT

In a world where everyone can have a voice (and an immediate, trusting network of friends and peers), the reputation of your business can be incredibly difficult to manage—especially if your business is in the wrong, or when there are misconceptions about your business that have been left unresolved. However, first of all it is important to distinguish the type of source of any issue, as it may not be something that is appropriate for the public relations department of your business to try to resolve, and it may be an issue that can be resolved by the customer service department much more effectively.

One of the first steps to understanding how to deal with reputation management is creating a decision tree based on certain factors that will help determine which department within your business is best equipped to deal with the issue—so a planning meeting is needed with the following departments to discuss the process for resolving these types of issues:

- Customer service—most likely the issue has started from a negative customer experience.
- Human resources—the issue may have arisen from an employee or ex-employee.
- Marketing—the issue may be an issue with the brand or business marketing function.

Once this decision tree has been agreed, the next factor to take into account with reputation management is the short-term and long-term effects of a negative online reputation. Most frequently these issues are expressed on blogs or forums (which are present in search engine results pages), or Twitter (which is not present in search engine results pages)—while negative comments on Twitter may spread quickly and reach a large volume of people, within days the comments have all but disappeared and the furore will have died down, blogs and forums, however, have a much longer-term impact on brand reputation. With something as sensitive as reputation, the most important factor is resolving the issue first, and then trying to ensure that the issue either fades away, away from sight of potential new customers, or that it is resolved in a very public way, so that if a new customer was to find the content, they would also find that the business has resolved the problem quickly and appropriately.

The most important part of reputation management in social spaces is either response or resolution—where the business has been misrepresented, a response may be necessary, depending on the situation, where there is someone who feels genuinely wronged, a timely resolution is necessary.

Reputation management in a negative situation can be incredibly difficult to deal with as it requires multiple departments to work in tandem to resolve the issue, but again, one of the main motivations for becoming a social business is so that this sort of collaboration can happen without barriers. As discussed in previous chapters, your business no longer operates within the four walls of your headquarters and there are both employees and consumers who can help to provide balance in the case of your business being mis-represented online—you just have to have an understanding of the network dynamics and the relationships to empower ambassadors.

CORPORATE SOCIAL RESPONSIBILITY

Corporate social responsibility has developed over the last ten years from being an exercise in public relations to an absolute necessity for almost any business, due partly to lobbying from action groups, and partly due to businesses having to demonstrate that they have a positive role in society aside from providing jobs and paying taxes. We are currently in the age of the ethically conscious business and the rise in access to technology now means that consumers can find out more information about your business than ever before—so creating flimsy corporate social responsibility projects that project vanity, rather than ethical mindedness, are increasingly being exposed both online and in the mainstream media.

It is important for the leadership team in your business to recognize the risks involved to your corporate reputation if you choose to ignore the importance of corporate social responsibility. However, if your business can prove the value of its role in society and align its behavior with the expectation set by a variety of different stakeholders, from customers and industry influencers, to the government and your business's investors, and communicate this clearly, it can become the best practice example for the industry and earn the stakeholder trust and reputational benefits that go with it.

There are a number of ways in which your business can use social technologies to help achieve this, from using social platforms to share information about your activity as socially responsible organization to engaging in conversations with influencers from a variety of backgrounds to help to shape government policy, encourage collaboration and enhance organizational transparency—bringing the walls down on your business.

CREATING AN INTEGRATED APPROACH TO CORPORATE SOCIAL RESPONSIBILITY

The leadership and public relations departments will, undoubtedly, already have plenty of information on the corporate issues that face your business—as part of both departments role, they have to be prepared for the business to be interrogated by the media, action groups and regulatory bodies—and this is a great place to start to begin to build a picture of the types of issues that surround your business, as well as being able to use this information to create a corporate social responsibility strategy for how your business plans to either resolve these issues or help demonstrate the value that it adds to society.

Using this information as a foundation, your business can then launch an online research project to determine the issues that the market believes face your business from a social or ethical point of view, establish an understanding of which action groups have identified your business as lacking a corporate social responsibility, and identify potential partners and influential voices that you can work alongside to resolve any potential issues and demonstrate your business's social conscience.

This research project should look to determine the following information:

- What do consumers associate with your business at a corporate level?
- How do online influencers perceive your business at a corporate level?
- What is the volume of conversation around your business at a corporate level?
- Are your existing corporate social responsibility activities viewed as a success? What is the current sentiment around these conversations?
- Who influences the conversation around corporate social responsibility in your sector? What size audience do they have?
- What corporate social responsibility practices are your competitors currently employing? Do they involve social technology?
- What key themes emerge from corporate social responsibility conversations in general? What is currently in the corporate social responsibility zeitgeist?
- Which organizations are currently demonstrating best practice in integrated corporate social responsibility?

The final report will then provide support in establishing the objectives and basic foundations for your business's integrated corporate social responsibility strategy.

CRISIS COMMUNICATIONS

We have already briefly touched on the "social media crisis" in previous chapters, but let us now look at the wider context for crisis communications and how social technology can be used to both react to issues, and manage those issues with sensitivity. Crises can arise from offline or online situations, but both can have potentially devastating effects on your business's reputation (especially in search, as outlined above), so understanding how social technology can help to keep things under control and calm a potential crisis situation is critical to a business's reputation.

Many of the processes that I have outlined in this chapter can help to stem a crisis situation; from having strong relationships with your market and the influencers within it (both old and new media) to understanding how news spreads across the community; all of these play a role in understanding how to control and manage a crisis situation that spreads to online media.

There are a few hygiene factors that we must clear up before getting into the actually process for managing a crisis. There are certain things that have to be created or set up in order to (1) be alerted to a potential crisis, and (2) understand who needs to be involved in the management process. The following are absolutely mandatory for any social business:

- A combination of social media monitoring tools that collect data in real time and have the ability to report (either via email or text message) spikes in mentions or combinations of certain keywords being used—this is a way of creating a sort of Google Alerts of steroids system.
- An escalation chart to understand the process and people that need to be involved in the event of an issue arising—this needs to be as lean as possible, as time is always of the essence in these situations.
- A series of FAQ and Q&A documents that have been developed from the same traditional public relations documents, but that have been tailored to an online audience.
- You must have a relationship with a number of influencers within your industry.
- A place for your brand to publish content that can then be linked to from third-party platforms.

Once these have all been created and put in place, your business is in a much stronger position to manage a crisis that spreads to online media. The process for identifying a potential social media crisis is as follows:

- Potentially negative content is flagged by your media or social media monitoring service, and immediately sent to a nominated member of the public relations department.
- The content is then analyzed through a number of different factors:
  - ☐ Where does the content fit on a scale of negativity?
  - ☐ What is the reach of the publisher?
  - ☐ What influence is the content likely to have on search engine results around your brand?
  - ☐ Is there an appropriate response from the business?
- Does the business have any relationships with influencers who may be able to help to defend the business?
- The public relations team then identifies the most appropriate owned media on which to publish a response.
- Content is drafted, approved and then published—with the influencers your business have relationships with then hopefully linking to that content.
- The situation is then very closely and carefully monitored.

There are no templates for managing a crisis through social media, but I have employed the process outlined above numerous times in situations of various levels of crisis. The most important thing to understand is tone of voice; if your business is in the wrong, be humble, if your business is being unfairly accused, be respectful but firm.

CONCLUSION

By this point you are going to be either terrified about the public relations aspect of social business or excited. I personally hope that it is the latter. Having started my career in public relations, I know how daunting conversations with people that influence your whole market can be, but I also quickly realized that once you can identify the types of content and conversations that those influencers (either online or offline) are interested in, it becomes a much more mutually beneficial relationship. One of the main things to avoid as a social business is being worried about reputation management and crisis communications—both have bad press because of a few overblown case studies where brands have taken a beating online, but so long as your business is prepared (or at least as prepared as it can be) and it is adhering to the principles laid out through this whole book (remember how many times I have reiterated the importance of being open and honest as a business—this is why) then your business should hold steady whatever issues arise.

The main point to take from this chapter is that there has been a shift in the types of media that influence your market—the traditional media is still incredibly important and valuable to businesses, it is just that social technology also adds in additional influencers to that group, as well as adding social data in that then drives the media agenda.

Hopefully by now you will be starting to understand why becoming a social business and understanding social data is so important—when Big Data is effectively driving the national news agenda, and tweets are being read out on the evening news, it is time to look at the converged world and figure out how your business can be part of it.

CHAPTER 9

Sales

There are, frankly, too many bad examples of businesses trying to use social technology to sell products directly to consumers. From small businesses looking to make a quick buck and an easy sale, to massive businesses with an old-school and hard-sell sales team—most social platforms now have their fare share of the Internet's equivalent of the door-to-door salesman. However, in keeping with convergence, these sales people are bad sales people offline as well as online, and those that are the opposite can sell incredibly well by building trust and influence within relevant communities.

Your sales force need to become part business ambassador, part expert in their field and part customer relationship manager. Online communities react well to people that know their industry and products inside out, and a large element of building trust with these communities is adding value. This value could come in the form of free advice, or a product trial, but the most important thing is building trust. Once members of your sale force have started to build a reputation for being reliable and honest, that is when referrals and sales will begin. This is not necessarily a direct sales relationship, but a way into a peer-recommendation—which we know from research is more powerful than a direct approach.

In my experience, there are two approaches to sales through social technology:

REACTIVE SALES

With millions of conversations taking place on social platforms every day, many of these mention brands, products and services directly—people looking for the best deal, advice, or additional information surrounding the product or service. These people are actively seeking help, not necessarily an immediate purchase, but they are already at the top of the sales funnel. If you sales force can find these people (more details to follow), they can provide assistance and advice that will help guide people toward the right purchase. It is important that your sales force has the most up to date information on your products or services possible, and that they are in a position to deliver advice that adds value to the customer experience (there is more detail on this later in the chapter).

However, it is also important to recognize that in an open and transparent organization, the right purchase might not be from your business—recommending an alternative is a sure fire way to demonstrate trust and honesty—it might hurt the month's sales figures and upset the head of acquisition, but in the long run it will build trust, and more importantly, it provides us with another data point—why was the alternative product more suitable? Is there something that your product development team can do to improve your product? Or, if your business is prepared to be agile and responsive, could you deliver the same product, but at a lower price or higher quality? Your sales force is on the front line of engagement with new customers and this is a great place to gain insights into your products or services.

PROACTIVE SALES

Give your sales force time to embed themselves in communities online, allow them to talk freely about the category that your business operates in and people will start to respect and value their opinions. Proactive sales are not necessarily direct sales, they could be referrals that travel quickly through the online networks we looked at in earlier chapters. Word of mouth online is easy to generate providing that you offer something of value. If your sales force is seen to be engaging regularly with a series of different people, it is demonstrating two things; (1) expertise within the category, and (2) a willingness to speak directly with the community. Two powerful tools that shine brightly in social spaces.

MOBILIZING THE SALES TEAM

Working directly with the sales team can be difficult, so starting to incorporate social technology into their regular routine will involve training, guidelines and guidance. The usual response to incorporate new technology into this type of department is that this is going to hurt their sales figures—but as we have previously covered, you need to be able to demonstrate to the department that integrating social technology into the sales function can reduce overheads, increasing the volume of customers that your sales team can speak to, and reduce the cost-per-acquisition.

TESTING, TRAINING AND RECRUITMENT

Using social technology to make sales is not about closing down the call centers or stop sales visits to new customers, it is about looking at how you can trial the use of social technology to enable the team to build a case for it to be incorporated across the whole team. Start the process by identifying no more than 1 percent of your sales force to begin using social technology—this way overall sales are less likely to take a direct hit and the leadership team can see this as a soft launch, rather than a potentially detrimental wide-scale roll out. This also allows you to trial the receptiveness of your market to being sold to in different space—it might be that if you are selling high-end sports cars that there is a lack of trust in making large purchases through social channels, equally, you may find that the market is much more receptive because they have more time to learn about your products and services, and the expertise of your employees.

If your business is to become truly social, then the employees recruited to be part of the social sales team need to be experienced and senior—remember, you are trying to build a business case for rolling out social technology across the whole team, so try to avoid bringing in junior and inexperienced sales employees. A senior member of the sales team should be overlooking the social sales team and they are going to need a direct line of contact into an experienced social media manager who can provide advice and guidance on how to approach people online appropriately.

After the team has been assembled, the whole social sales team need to be put through a formal social media training course to give them the confidence and skills to be comfortable (and look comfortable) using social technology and communicating in this space. This should take between half a day and a day and the following topics are absolutely mandatory for the training session.

- A general introduction to social media and technology.
- An introduction to this specific project, outlining the objectives, strategy and implementation.

- A detailed explanation of the guidelines that have been set, the integration process between other departments within the business, and the process for completing sales.
- A guide to locating leads using social monitoring tools (with hands-on demonstrations of each tool that is to be used).
- A channel guide (giving hands-on demonstrations of each appropriate social platform).
- A guide to reporting.
- Case studies of successful implementations of social sales.
- Example scenarios and best case responses.

FINDING LEADS

There are a selection of free tools that can be run in parallel to capture comments made on social platforms that indicate a potential lead. While these tools will not guarantee that you capture every lead, they should be able to track at least the majority. These include (but are by no means limited to):

- TweetDeck: TweetDeck is a simple desktop application that allows users to create multiple searches around keywords, the application then collects any tweets that use those keywords. Be careful to carefully structure your keyword searches though so as to really hone down on tweets that matter to your business.
- Google Alerts: This service from Google will email you when certain keywords are found on new content. The service covers blog content, some forum content, and anything appearing in Google News—it is however, far from comprehensive.
- BoardReader: This is a simple service that lets you search forums specifically using keyword strings, and then subscribe to an RSS feed of the search results, which update hourly, alerting you to any new content that is posted mentioning your keywords.

(RSS feeds are "pipes" of content that you can send into an RSS feed reader, such as Google Reader. The feed reader will then display all new content on a one-page dashboard—so instead of having to visit multiple websites to check for new content, it is all sent to one place for you to read.)

SCALE

As with all departments, scaling the social sales team is not going to happen overnight, and building the business case for investing more resource is going to have to be proven over time. However, once the tills are ringing and the cost reductions are becoming more and more evident, this type of social technology can then start being built into the whole department. This is an important marker in the process of becoming truly social as a business, but the potential rewards far outweigh the initial investment. Once your social sales team has started to feel comfortable in this space it can expect to:

- Increase sales.
- Increase reputation (through demonstrating expertise in the category).
- Improve cross-selling, through stronger relationships with the market.
- Improve the customer journey, through smart integration.
- Identify new markets through research and insight.
- Increase positive word of mouth.
- Reduce overheads in the sales department.
- Increase overall profitability "per head."

The last point usually has the most resonance with the leadership function, as sales departments can be incredibly, but are obviously an absolute pre-requisite to actually selling anything, so any significant increase in sales or reduction in costs that can be achieved is going to have a profound impact on the business as whole.

CUSTOMER EXPERIENCE

Enhancing the customer experience breaches the boundary between many business disciplines; customer service, public relations, marketing and research and development. Yet this is probably one of the most efficient ways to improve a customer relationship and begin to cross-sell products through some basic thought-leadership. This is the point at which integration becomes massively important, so it is important for an interdepartmental working group to be created to plot the true customer journey and understand how this maps back against the way in which your organization is set up—rather than the traditional route of creating a customer journey based on your organization. Understand the behavior first, then create the structure.

TRACKING

Tracking sales made through social technology can be difficult—there is not always a linear progression from, say, a conversation on Twitter between the sales force and a prospective customer, and a call that comes into the sales team a few weeks later. There are, however, a few ways to improve this.

■ When linking to content, always use unique trackable links—there are professional versions of bit.ly, and your IT or digital department may also have a bespoke linking tool. These links can also be tied into analytics tools such as Google Analytics and Omniture, giving you a little more detail as to the behavior of the prospective customer (while this can be a nightmare to track thousands of unique URLs, it can provide an incredible level of insight into behavior, and the approach of the sales person—allowing the sales force to become much more agile in its approach to selling through social technologies).

■ If the sales force is building relationships with prospective new customers, a simple request for if they engaged with anyone within the organisation on a social platform will help track their progress through the sales funnel, and help attribute social technology's involvement in that process.

■ As well as using unique URLs, tracking traffic from social platforms onto an eCommerce site will start to give an indication of the progress of the trial.

■ Finally, the sales force themselves can process the sale—taking a conversation either onto the phone or onto email—this is obviously the most reliable way of tracking sales!

CHANNEL STRATEGY

Choosing the right channels to use for customer acquisition can be challenging, as most people use different networks for different purposes—but the most important thing is to focus on the conversation rather than the channel. If your sales team works with the Chief Data Officer and customer service department, then you can begin to understand the behaviors of existing customers and build on that—however, it is still incredibly important to look outside of the customer base for cues on which platforms are going to serve the best purpose for a sales message. With this in mind, there are certain data that can be collected through a small audit project. This can be carried out in co-ordination with the aforementioned departments, and a lot of the data should already exist, however the following should be addressed:

In terms of potential new customers:

Reactive sales
- Which platforms are being used to discuss your products and services mentioned directly in a sales situation?
- What is the volume of these conversations?
- What is the sentiment?
- How does the community react to these conversations? What is the general sentiment of the reactions?
- What types of themes are mentioned around these conversations?

Proactive sales
- Which platforms are being used to discuss the category in which your products and services sit?
- What is the volume of these conversations in comparison to reactive mentions?
- What is the sentiment for the category as whole?
- What is the share of voice among your competitors?
- How does the community react to these conversations? What is the general sentiment of the reactions?
- What types of themes are mentioned around these conversations?

Once this project has been completed, the sales team will then be in a much stronger position to begin formulating a channel strategy that is based on pure insight, rather than gut instinct or experience.

READING THE SOCIAL SITUATION

Understanding the need states of your customers is obviously incredibly important, but it is also important to acknowledge the social situation that they are currently in at the point of a mention of your products or services or category. Understanding mood and context is absolutely fundamental to approaching a new prospect and should not, under any circumstances, be misread—this may lead to an incredibly negative experience with your business. For example, if someone has just found out that their car has failed its MOT test and they are in an emotional state of distress, then it is probably not the right time to contact them regarding an offer that your business has on car exhausts. Selling through social technology is about being social and your sales team has to possess a certain level of social awareness. This can also be augmented with social data around the types of state that your market are usually in—whether they sit within an emotional or rational space—that will then help to build a sales message house that fits perfectly with the market.

The days of sales people sounding like QVC presenters are long gone—the market is demanding honesty, openness and humanness and it is absolutely integral that your sales team understands this. However, when training the sales team in how to sell through social technology, allow them to create their own tone of voice—after all, their tone of voice is theirs, so that is how they are going to feel most natural talking to people, and that will help to build stronger, more long-term relationships with your market.

AFTER-SALES CARE AND ONGOING RELATIONSHIPS

There is a difficult cross-over between the sales team and the customer service team in the sense that once a relationship has been built with a new customer, who inside the business, "owns" that relationship? This is where running an open business becomes integral to ensuring relationships have longevity. The sales department has to have an open and ongoing dialogue with the customer service department, as well as access to the social customer relationship management system (more on that later), and the social sales team has to be able to introduce new people into the relationship that are then involved in the after-sales care of each customer. This is not to say that the sales team must then disappear, on the contrary, it is then the responsibility of both departments to ensure that the customer is happy and content with their direct lines of communication into the business. No department should drop the relationship, instead work together, integrated, to give that individual relationship the most attention and provide the most value possible.

PROVIDING REAL VALUE

One frequent flaw in businesses trying to sell products and services through social technology is the rush to provide "social media only" sales promotions. I personally have two issues with providing real value through social media; (1) your sales promotion strategy should not have promotions that are costly just for social platforms (see below), and (2) providing real value should come from expertise and advice first, then sales promotions later. Too many businesses hide their expertise away, when this could potentially be massively valuable to the market—monetize your expertise and give that away for free, then your business will be in much better shape to charge the correct price for its actual services and products. Do not sell your products and services short, instead use the expertise that you wrap around them anyway to demonstrate the value your products and services provide.

GROUP-BUYING AND DEALS

Since the launch of GroupOn and similar group-buying services, businesses have been quick to look at the value and profitability in these types of sales, however, there are two massive considerations to be made before doing any of this type of activity.

- Is the activity aimed at awareness and trial, rather than profitability? Many of the businesses that use group-buying platforms use them for raising awareness and "getting people through the door," rather than a boost to revenue—and as such, the deals are usually loss-making. Those businesses that tried to alter their business model to deliver group-buying have been hurt, as the margins needed make profitability (even at large scale) very difficult.
- Is the activity going to harm your reputation in the market and make your products and services look "cheap"? A fire sale on your products and services may seem like a great way to raise awareness and generate trial, but should your business cut price points to do so? The psychology behind price points (as mentioned in Jonah Lehrer's *How We Decide*) means that if you sell a product at a reduced rate and the experience is bad, the market will expect much more from your products if the price suddenly rises back to its original state again.

There are countless examples of group-buying and discounting that have worked incredibly well, but always consider the strategy and objectives behind this type of sales promotion—it might be unnecessarily hurting your business's reputation when giving product trials to influential voices could potentially give you a much bigger (and more trusted) sales boost.

SOCIAL SALES PRINCIPLES

There are six principles that I believe a business should adhere to when starting to use social technology for customer acquisition:

- If you want to sell through social platforms, your sales force has to know your product, business and category inside out.
- Always act transparently, letting people know where you work and what you do early on in the conversation—the last thing that you want a community to think is that you are trying to trick them. The majority of the time, this can be easily done through including this information on a profile page, or biography section.
- Tracking is absolutely integral to both making the sale and measuring the impact that social technology has had—helping to build an internal business case for selling through social platforms.
- Do not see the final sale as the final goodbye—if you have built a relationship with a community, continue to communicate and add value—it will build your reputation and influence while also displaying an openness that most businesses are afraid of.
- Reactive sales are the low hanging fruit, but proactive sales offer more longevity—receiving personal referrals from within a community is a very strong indication that your sales force is building a reputation online.
- Provide value, advice and honesty at all times. This seems like such a simple principle to follow, yet it is the one thing that people get wrong time and time again.

CONCLUSION

It is important to avoid just letting sales people sell, instead a much more effective way of starting the sales process is by giving your whole organization a voice. It may be that one of your most experienced employees does not work on the sales team, yet they can provide incredible insight into the category and products that the sales team could not provide—ensure that there is a direct line of communication between these people (who are likely to already have a reputation and influence online) and your sales team, that way once a conversation has been started that looks like it may end in a sale, the more experienced employee can make a smooth introduction to one of the sales team.

CHAPTER 10

Research and Development

For your business to make money, you must put people first. Any business that sets out to make people want its product rather than make a product that people want will wrap its organization in process, models, empirical research and economies of scale in search of millions in turnover, rather than enriching the lives of the people that are actually buying the product. If we put people first, and enrich their lives, make things easier, or more beautiful, then profits will follow. This is the most important ethic of modern, successful business, and as we know, we can use raw data from social technologies to actually make products that people want to buy. So how should the modern research and development department start to integrate social data, technology and thinking into its every day practice? First, the department must learn to stop striving for perfection, as Taleb states in his collection of aphorisms, "We love imperfection, the right kind of imperfection; we pay up for original art and typo-laden first editions."[1]

The days of the research and development team being locked in a darkened laboratory are numbered.

RESEARCH

The role of the research and development team is to create new product concepts, or improve existing products and take them from concept to the final product—both stages have, historically, employed traditional research methods to confirm the viability, and then functionality of the concept, but then putting the product or service into mass production. As with strategic planning in marketing, we can use data from social technologies to improve this process, helping to uncover previously unknown insights from niche online media, listening to raw product feedback online through influencer groups, and testing the concepts as they move through the development cycle, gaining valuable feedback as the product gets closer to production. There are five key areas of research that I believe that the department could start generating insights from with almost immediate effect:

New product development

Creativity around new concepts does not have to be born in the research and development lab, as there are hundreds of forums and blogs around almost every industry that are filled with members who are speaking about new ideas and product concepts every day. These people are experts within their industry and often come from the industry itself, academia, the media, or from the position of super fans. This type of activity is most prevalent in the technology and science sectors, but the behavior is also replicated in fields as diverse as pharmaceuticals, right through to architecture. Your business's product development can spend time in these social spaces, either contributing or watching the conversations take place, gaining valuable insights and sparking creativity that may have otherwise been hidden.

Competitor research

While market research and competitor analysis is carried out at various levels of product development (from research and development, right through to customer care and marketing)—the critical point for this research is before a product has been put into production. Using the same techniques outlined in the chapter on marketing and advertising, it is possible to find people talking online about the industry and your business's competitors, and the research and development team can use this information to improve existing products (where faults are exposed in competitor products, the team can ensure the same faults do not befall your products), or build the feedback into the concept stage for new product development (as outlined above).

Sourcing expertise

Regardless of the industry your business operates in, there are times when expertise at this critical level is difficult to source and sacrifices have to be made. However, if your research and development team are actively listening and participating in the types of conversations outlined above, then approaching experts in those social spaces is going to prove easy to achieve, and the decision to hire certain people can be made safe in the knowledge that they have demonstrated their expertise and influence in the online space.

Human insights

Outside of the expert and "super fan" spaces online, the rest of the web is awash with consumers discussing the different benefits and drawbacks to products and services across all industries. The department can work alongside the Chief Data Officer to start incorporating these mass human insights into the planning and development of new and existing products.

"Labs" powered by social technology

Lastly, for concept research and insights, is "Labs" powered by social technology. The idea behind the social media lab is simple; you take a sample of your superfans (these can be sourced from anywhere, such as Facebook (the most engaged users), Social CRM (your most loyal customers who have a presence on social platforms), communities and forums (as mentioned above—the experts), influential media and bloggers (as identified by the marketing and public relations departments), there are a myriad of ways to recruit people), and test out different concepts and product propositions with them—asking both quantitative and qualitative questions and gathering insights on a daily basis. Most businesses reward this type of research, but most superfans will want to be involved in the project because they feel loved by the business. These sorts of projects can be run a number of ways, but a great example is the way in which Unilever uses Facebook in its VIP labs program—users register to be part of the program, and then they are asked for their opinions on any one of 11 different Unilever products (including brands like PG Tips and Persil). Consumers are then rewarded with early access to new products, discounts on products and invitations to events that Unilever is holding.

IDENTIFYING COMMON PRODUCT/SERVICE FLAWS

Through similar research methods outlined above, and again, working alongside the Chief Data Officer, the research and development team can quickly discover consistent reports of flaws in the products or services that it creates. Social platforms act as an early warning system for these types of issues as consumer, and if we can track where these types of comments are left regularly for our industry, we can resolve the issues (hopefully) quickly, and if not, we can announce a product recall before the mainstream and trade media has discovered that there is a story. Then, it is possible to use the same information contained in the complaints we found online to look at how the product can be improved.

TESTING AND TRIALS

Using focus groups and ethnographic studies to test concept products has been around for decades, however social technology now enables research and development teams to add to this research by using online influencers and existing consumers that are discussing the business and its products online and incorporate them into the testing and trials too. The benefit of adding social data into the testing phase is that you can be highly specific when choosing who to invite into the test—so you can split test groups into minute detail, and use social platforms to talk to them on a daily basis—giving the research group greater access to the test groups. The department can also (if it chooses to) begin to build a community of these testers, by inviting them into a closed group on a platform such as Facebook, or a password protected forum.

As well as carrying out standard consumer tests, the research and development team can also choose to test with superfans and industry influencers too. By working alongside the Chief Data Officer, the marketing department and the public relations department, the team can identify use social data to find brand superfans (for example, if you take the top 1% of engaged fans on your business or product's Facebook page—these are the people that are driving conversations on Facebook about your business or product) and influencers (these are likely to be the same influencers that the public relations and marketing departments are inviting to events and sending products to already). This type of testing allows for a much broader set of results, and helps to include more people in the development of your business's products—breaking the walls of your business down and inviting in the community.

CREDITING THE COMMUNITY

If your department has been working closely with a community of consumers which has been helping and advising on product development, even at a basic level, it is important to acknowledge the community's contribution to the development of that product—especially if that specific feature or suggestion goes into final production. The best way to think about crediting the community is to see the project as a KickStarter project. KickStarter is an America service that allows budding entrepreneurs and inventors to "pitch" their idea on the KickStarter site—people can then choose to "back" projects by making a small investment (usually a micro-investment), then, once the idea has reached a certain level of investment it will go into production and everyone that chose to invest in it receives a product. So, while your research and development team is not taking financial investment to help develop products and services, it is taking a time and expertise investment from the community—and when you put this into a wider context, this is saving the business a small fortune in numerous product iterations, product research and testing—credit where credit is due.

The way in which these ideas are credited, however, does not have to be financial, or even based on sending the final product to the people who helped develop it (although in my mind that is one of the best ways of crediting contributors). For many experts and influencers, a name check in a company blog post, or recognition at a launch event will be enough kudos to keep them happy—it is important to remember that many of these niche communities run on ego—being the first to an idea, having the best idea, or the most innovative solution, is the social currency of choice for forums—this is simple group dynamics, but everyone in that forum is looking for peer recognition. If you recognize the contribution that they made, it is worth some serious social currency.

OPEN SOURCE YOUR PRODUCTS

One of the most challenging concepts in modern product development is the idea of having "open source" products. Until recently it was mainly used in software development, but this way of developing and launching products is fast becoming acceptable in lots of different industries (notably Pharmaceuticals and mobile telecommunications). The concept behind the term is simple; once a product or service has been developed, it is launched and the "blueprints" of that product are released into the wider community for people to redevelop, improve on and learn from—effectively showing the world how you make your products and services.

"Open source" as a concept has been around for more than a hundred years—it first came to use in 1911 in America when a regulatory body broke up a monopolistic market that had formed around a certain type of car engine (the 2-stroke engine, in case you were wondering), the regulatory body then took the production and design blueprints and effectively barred them from being patented, and encouraged car manufacturers to share more information with their competitors—to massive success.

The challenges that business's face from having "open source" products today are numerous; not only is the business going to worry about competitors replicating its products, but it is also going to worry about consumers replicating them too. However, the benefits behind "open source" products, in my opinion, far outweigh the potential drawbacks. Once your product has been launched, it is already on the market, so competitors will struggle to displace it if they simply replicate the production. If they begin to try to innovate the design, the responsibility lies with your research and development department, which should have already started looking at how to innovate the product since its launch, and (if your business is truly a social business) the innovation will be coming from the community that is using that product or service—keeping your business ahead of its competitors, even when you give them the blueprints to your products.

Where this type of production really comes alive is when you give product blueprints to your industry communities. The same superfans and experts that we discussed earlier will play around with the design, tinker with the genetics of your product and create new blueprints, splintering your product into thousands of variations. It is at this point that the research and development department can start looking over each of this variations and figuring out if any of them make for viable consumer products. There are numerous examples of this type of work from digital businesses such as Spotify, which has a section on its website dedicated to community driven "hacks" that utilize the Spotify API (limited access to the product, but open source in a sense) and wrap new layers of features around the original product—and Spotify publishes all of the useful "hacks" on its website.

SCALING SOCIAL TECHNOLOGY

One of challenges with testing new products and improvements made to other products is scale and budget—market research is expensive and can take time. Using social technology allows the research and development department to easily scale tests—with such a huge pool of potential test groups, multiple tests can run across different products and services at the same time, in different closed communities, all sending insight and data through in a constant stream of feedback.

CONCLUSION

Research and development has always been insights-driven and steeped in consumer testing, and social technology does not need to change that, but it can add to it. The products and services that businesses sell need to deliver on consumer wants and needs, rather than sit in beautiful packaging waiting to disappoint a customer because they have bought into the brand, rather than the product. I have already mentioned it twice before, but when it comes to the future of product research and development, I'm reminded of John Wilshire's fantastic quote:

Make things people want, don't make people want things.

The point that John is making is that businesses now have so much access to data from, and conversations with our market that, as a business, there is really is not an excuse to be producing commoditised, over-branded factory fodder any more. Even simple implementations of social technology can make a massive difference to a department such as research and development—this is the room where the butterfly effect is really going to have an impact on the business, if the insights are wrong, it affects everything in the business. I am by no means implying that by adding social data and insights into the process that every product is going to be a sell-out, but what I am trying to say is that by adding additional market data, that is, from the people that buy, discuss and already influence your products, you are narrowing the chances of failure.

CHAPTER 11

Human Resources

As your business starts to implement certain principles to become a social business, one aspect which is key to making the transition is human resources. Understanding how your employees behave, both internally and externally, is absolutely paramount to being able to build a stronger workforce that has a much deeper relationship with your business, building loyalty, promoting knowledge sharing, and increasing internal understanding of what the business stands for—ultimately, this should improve morale, employee retention, and your employee's ability to sell your business to prospective customers much more effectively.

Creating an open, social business brings with it a lot of risk and empowering your workforce to speak almost limitlessly (and without corporate control) about your business can be a daunting prospect for both the organization *and* employees. However, there are a few key things that your human resources department can do in order to minimize the risk for both parties. These include:

- Employee conversation guidelines
  Almost all businesses will have a staff handbook that gives historical background information on the company, details of the leadership team, product information, and so on. In a social business, this handbook should contain information on what being an open, social business means. It should include information on:
  - ☐ The principles that your business adheres to as a social business.
  - ☐ The different audiences online that matter to your business (with a link to download an RSS feed of their blogs/forums so your employees can read the content that these people publish about your industry).
  - ☐ A comprehensive guide to how you can talk about your work, your colleagues and your employee online.

- [ ] An escalation chart detailing who to contact when an issue occurs—make this as simple as possible.
- [ ] Information on legal matters relating to online activity (for the potentially serious issues around things like libel and defamation).
- [ ] Direct contact information for people within the business that can offer advice and guidance.
- [ ] A list of dos and do nots—keep these minimal, and promote common sense above anything.
- [ ] A link to the central social data monitoring system, with details about what the information means and how it can be used.
- [ ] A collection of useful links that will help employees to boost their knowledge about being part of a social business.

- Ensuring employees have access to all business information (both internal and external)
  - [ ] If your business is to communicate more efficiently across departmental silos, then access to internal information and knowledge is key—having a central library or hub, held on an intranet will help this, but also sharing information about each other is also important. One of the aspects of IBM's business that makes it so successful is its ability to create working groups of people with highly complementary skill sets and experience—your business can move toward this by sharing individual employee skills on an intranet, allowing other employees that are in need of help the ability to find someone within the business that can help, and finding them quickly.
  - [ ] If your employees have an Internet connection, there is a strong chance that they will already be reading external information that relates to your industry—from Googling competitors, to hearing rumors in forums—this type of media consumption is already taking place. One of the opportunities for the business is to encourage this—improving knowledge around your market, products and audience across the whole workforce can only be beneficial, and encourage people to share the links and content that they find useful—it may even be useful to create an internal bookmarking tool that allows people to "tag" content online easily and then share it to a newsfeed displayed on

an intranet (there are numerous other methods for this type of sharing, including group email addresses, corporate micro-blogging tools like Yammer, and (very old school, I know) wiki tools).

- Social business mentoring schemes
  - ☐ As part of becoming a social business, there is going to be a certain element of helping employees make the transition too—as your business starts the transition, the leadership team should create a group of "social business mentors," people that have experience and knowledge of working with social technology and are able to see beyond the marketing function. These people can then support different members of staff, sharing experience and helping your employees to see the role that social technology plays in both their role and how it affects the business as a whole.
- Workshops and training
  - ☐ Whether you work with a consultancy, or an in-house team of specialists to begin to make the transition to becoming a social business, one of the most important aspects is going to be training the whole workforce in how, why, when, and what to do with social technology in their day to day work, as well as explaining the business's vision, and how social technology is going to help achieve that vision.
- Monitoring
  - ☐ As I outlined earlier, the role of the data in the business cannot be underestimated, it is the foundation from which we can build a social business. It also allows us to track employee conversations that relate to the business and industry in general. By reviewing which employees have social media profiles (it should be a voluntary decision to provide them, might I add) and combining this with online monitoring should allow you to comprehensively monitor for any potential issues that might arise from empowering your employees to talk on behalf of your on social platforms.
- Feedback and evaluation
  - ☐ Understanding and skills sets for social technology are constantly having to be adapted, with technology changing on a daily basis, with this in mind it is important to

encourage ongoing learning within the organization and work this into employee evaluation and performance feedback.

INTERNAL COMMUNICATIONS

Internal communications is an integral part of building a social business—communicating with your employees, helping them to communicate with each other, and communities outside of your business will all work together to help everyone to feel like they are part of the fabric of the business—to feel like they understand the business, and that they make a difference. There are numerous aspects to internal communications, and a book could be written about it alone, but what I have tried to outline below an approach for building an internal communications strategy and looked at different applications of social technology that should help in engaging more efficiently with your employees.

Building a strategy for communicating with your employees has to be done with the same rigor and attention to detail as communicating with your market—and the same type of approach can be applied that I outlined in Chapter 7. The communications plan needs to follow the same type of sales funnel, and while there is a different definition of *Conversion*, *Awareness* and *Engagement* retain the same definitions. Outlined below is a series of questions that will help your human resources department build an effective internal communications strategy.

Awareness—how can you raise awareness of information around your business?
- How do you plan to stimulate awareness using content and information?
- How do you plan on using different platforms to distribute types of media? Which platforms do you plan to use?
- Which elements of owned (intranets, content libraries etc.), earned (forums, blogs, wikis, etc.) and paid media (promotional materials, posters, print-outs, etc.) can act as attention grabbers for your employees?
- How do you plan on tracking traffic into the next phase of the funnel?

Engagement—how can you stimulate conversations between employees and the business?

- Once you have captured the attention of your employees and they are into the next phase of the funnel, how do you plan to stimulate conversations between the organization and other employees?
- Where do you plan to engage with the consumer? Is it a closed Facebook group? Or the discussions section of your intranet? How do you plan to amplify and reward the engagement to raise awareness among other employees?
- How are you going to encourage people to share content with other employees?
- Do you have a calendar for ongoing engagement?

Conversion—how do you create business and brand ambassadors out of your employees?

- If it is possible, how do you plan to incentivise the conversion?
- How do you plan to measure whether or not your employees have become ambassadors? Is it part of their appraisal, or could it be done through internal surveying?
- What is the next phase of engagement and how do you maintain their status as ambassadors?

This type of approach allows you to focus your attention on creating platforms that contribute to an end goal, rather than creating disparate platforms that have little coherence with each other. It also allows for detailed tracking and measurement, and using basic analytics and conversion models, you can set realistic KPIs on the activity too.

The next section of using social technology in internal communications looks at five different potential uses for social platforms and data within your organization, these are the five Cs: collaboration, change, crowdsourcing, community and communication flow. While each of the five areas will increase engagement, it is important to remember that these ideas may not necessarily work within your business—a lot depends on the culture of your organization.

Collaboration

Your business is filled with exceptionally talented people that have skills that most of your other employees do not even know about—how can you promote collaboration that defies departmental boundaries and fosters innovation? Collaboration has been in the business zeitgeist for at least the last 20 years, as businesses try to utilize the different skill sets of their employees to create smarter thinking and better ideas, if we follow Johnson's idea of the *Adjacent Possible*, then creativity thrives on both conflict between different experiences and exposure to different ways of thinking. However, many businesses have tried to foster a collaborative environment by designing open plan working spaces, "hot desking," and having corporate away days at which employees play rounders together. Collaboration needs to in the DNA of your business, it needs to be part of the everyday experience of your employees, rather than a once-a-year retreat to the countryside—and social technology can help to integrate this into the everyday.

Simple implementations of social technology can range from launching an internal forum where your business and its employees can post business challenges to be answered by anyone across the business, to creating an instant messaging system between different departments so that they can quickly communicate and collaborate on problems. However, if you would like to give this type of activity the optimum opportunity to succeed, there needs to be motivation—whether this is in the form of rewards for successful ideas, or recognition for contributions, there needs to be a motivating factor that pulls people into the conversation.

Change

The importance of internal communication in a time of change within the business should never be overlooked. There is a natural tendency for people to fear change as it sparks fears about the future of the business, the future of their department, and usually (more alarmingly) the future of their job. At a time of change, the leadership function needs to communicate what is changing, why it is changing, how it will be changing, when it will be changing and how it affects each and every employee.

There are simple ways to communicate these changes that avoid the trappings of cold, all-department emails, or flaccid brochures with stock images of happy employees on the front cover. At times of change, employees want to hear from the head of business what is happening—messaging passed through management structures far too often falls into whispers and rumors before reaching all of the employees, creating dissent and disinformation. If your business has a more than 100 employees, it is going to be a formidable task for the head of the business to talk to every employee in person. However, there are simple implementations of social technology that can resolve this problem, such as using a video livestreaming platform and enabling people to watch from all around the business, all around the world, and more powerful than this is the ability with most of these streaming services to allow questions to be sent in instantly through the livestreaming tool itself—giving your CEO or Managing Director the opportunity to answer questions and appease concerns live, and completely transparently.

There are, of course, obvious caveats to this and there will always be information that the business cannot disclose to the whole organization, but this type of change management can have a big impact on awareness and understanding, as well as loyalty and employee happiness.

Crowdsourcing

The term "crowdsourcing" (unsurprisingly) comes from the idea of sourcing ideas from a crowd of people, usually implemented by a business with its consumers or market, in order to find suggestions for new products, services or ideas—as covered in the previous chapter on research and development. This type of mass-idea generation has obvious applications from an internal communications perspective in terms of helping provide solutions to business problems (as outlined above in section on collaboration), but it can also be used as a tool for polling around different ideas. Let us look at an example; your business is currently undergoing a corporate "rebrand" and the branding agency has provided three different visuals for the rebrand. As well as putting the visuals into research groups and traditional testing methods, why not all so crowdsource opinions from your whole business? Your business is made of employees, but they are also consumers and (should hopefully) have a very firm understanding about what your brand stands for.

Community

We have previously discussed the role of personal connections over organizational hierarchy in Chapter 1 and these personal networks can be massively useful—both in harnessing existing connections, and in helping your employees to make new connections within your business. This can be achieved through simple community initiatives such as launching a company forum for people to speak to each other in. The benefit of launching this type of activity is that it can both increase efficiency in the workforce (by giving people a place to talk informally to each other, you are psychologically segregating that activity from other parts of the day when they may have spent time speaking to people in the communal kitchen), as well as increasing the strength of your workforce as a whole by making stronger bonds across different parts of your business—which then makes interdepartmental work a lot easier, as the personal boundaries of not knowing people in certain departments disappears.

It is important to define what this community should be for; it may be that it is simply an informal place to discuss anything, or it may be that it is to share interesting information with the rest of the business. The decision comes down to the type of culture your business has, and the business objectives identified when building the internal communications strategy. Whatever the objective, your community will need a moderator or community manager to stimulate conversations and help avoid any negativity such as arguing with one another or bullying.

There are a number of principles that your moderator/community manager should follow:

- Create a series of rules and regulations for the community to abide by.
- Stimulate conversations, do not capsize them.
- Make introductions between different people.
- Help to scale the community, introducing new sections and areas as the number of users grows.
- Help guide new employees through the basic guidelines and etiquettes of a community or forum.
- Moderate content that is deemed offensive or abusive, but explain why the content has been removed.

■ Capture, analyze and report usage data to the human resources department and the Chief Data Officer—using the data gathered to drive further innovation and insights within the business.

In the initial launch phase, and as the community starts to grow, this process should not be resource intensive. However, as the community grows larger (and return on investment is increasingly being proven), this will obviously become more resource intensive and will (eventually) require a full-time community manager.

Providing that your community fits within the wider internal communications strategy and that there are tangible benefits to the business, your organization should start to see some of those benefits quickly.

Communication flow

One common concern about adding additional internal communications channels into an already hectic communications structure is that the new channels are going to distract employees and generate additional workload, taking them away from doing their actual work. However, there are two factors that help debunk this myth.

■ Most organizations suffer from "email bloat"—because there is only one channel for communication, everything is funnelled through that single channel. However, if you can create a hierarchy of content and channel, you can massively reduce the strain placed on email inboxes across the business. This can be done on importance of content, urgency, or any other number of factors, but it basically helps to reduce the volume of Friday afternoon "funny cat" emails sent around the organization, allowing people to choose when they want to receive less-urgent, less-important communications.

■ The insinuation that improving internal communications and employee loyalty will be distracting for employees is, quite frankly, ludicrous. It is within the same frame as saying that television advertising distracts consumers from making a purchase. It does not, it enables the purchase, it enhances the experience, and the same can be said for internal communications.

RECRUITMENT

Social platforms are a goldmine for both recruitment agencies and human resources departments—with platforms like LinkedIn, and professional blogs enabling people to present their skills and experience to a mass audience, a lot of the vetting process and filtering can be done automatically without having to manually sort through CVs and have first interviews with people. The rise of social platforms has also produced a negative type of behavior from recruitment agencies and human resource departments—snooping on personal information. I am sure that anyone reading this book will be able to recall a story told to them by someone either looking to hire someone, or someone looking to be hired, of finding Facebook photos of the potential recruit looking a little worse for wear while on holiday, or having written an outrageous blog post years ago, and then not being hired on the back of the potential employer that information—with close to a billion people using Facebook and its privacy settings awkward to navigate, it is hardly difficult to find incriminating evidence on even the most angelic candidate. There are numerous moral and ethical issues attached to this practice, and I could propose the argument against it for another 10,000 words, but instead I would like to focus my attention on the reason you have purchased this book.

This book is about building a social business, creating an environment for both your market and employees to have a human conversation that is devoid of corporate speak and jargon, that relies on personal experiences and personality, rather than press releases and promotional marketing packs. The entirety of this book is aimed at making your business more human. So, when your human resources department refuses to hire a potential employee because they spent six months in Vietnam drinking and singing in karaoke bars and uploaded the photos to their Flickr account, this sets a precedent for your existing employees to become secretive about their activities outside of work, in case the same judgment is passed on them. A social, human business needs to be run by social and human people.

Well, now we have covered the negative side of recruitment using social technology, let us look at the more positive side. Reducing costs through using social data and networks to recruit people into your business. Using a recruitment agency can be expensive, especially when you are hiring at the senior end of the business, but much of the searching can be done through networks such as LinkedIn and personal online networks—then, once you have found a series of candidates, you can then use their professional profiles on social platforms and blogs to build a better picture of that person, before finally inviting them in for an actual face to face interview. This saves recruitment fees, reduces the chances of hiring the wrong person and massively reduces the amount of time it takes to locate potential new employees.

IT

Corporate information technology (IT) policies are usually notoriously stringent, which is usually driven by fears of security issues, potential misbehavior of employees, or an over-zealous (and damaging) focus on productivity. If your business is going to become more open and social, it is going to have to realize that many of the fears mentioned above are a hangover from the 1980s—treating your workforce like children is going to encourage them to act like children, yet giving them responsibility and rewarding them will see improvements in employee/employer trust and loyalty. If you make your employees feel that they are part of the fabric of your business, dissent and abuse of the business should see a big reduction.

Security fears have always been present in business—from keeping documents in a safe, to underground bomb-proof bunkers filled with servers—corporate security is an incredibly important part of retaining competitive advantage and maintaining the smooth running of the whole organization. However, since the rise of social networking sites like Facebook and Twitter, over-zealous management and IT departments have been putting these sites behind the corporate firewall to hamper any potential procrastination that employees might fall into. For a traditional business, with single points of communication to its market, this makes complete sense, except "traditional business" no longer exists. Your market wants to talk to your employees, and they are going to do that either within working hours or outside of them, but the best possible approach is to encourage and harness these conversations, rather than punish them—they can be incredibly powerful for your business, and rewarding employees for communicating with the market is much more effective than punishing them for it.

CONCLUSION

Implementing social technology into the human resources function can have a series of positive impacts on your business:

- It can boost employee engagement.
- It can create business and brand ambassadors of your employees.
- It can foster innovation and creativity.
- It can help your business to recruit people with better skills and a better cultural fit.
- It can help reduce recruitment costs, while improving retention of employees.

However, as always, the devil is in the details, and the human resources department of your business is going to have to adhere to certain principles if it hopes to achieve the objectives outlined above. These principles are simple in nature, but if they are not adhered to, it may hamper employee engagement, or worse, it may create friction your employees and the business itself. The principles are:

- Do not force employees into surrendering their social media profile information, encourage it.
- Give your employees a structure within which to engage with the market online, and be tolerant of mistakes—we are trying to create a more human business, and humans make mistakes.
- Reward and recognize those that actively contribute and collaborate, but do not persecute those that do not.
- Use social technology to reduce the burden of email overkill for your employees, do not maintain the same level of email communication and add in additional channels too!

As mentioned in almost every chapter in this book, the key to successful integration is avoiding making massive changes quickly, and making sure that the objectives, strategy and implementation fit within the structure and culture of your organization—just because certain implementations have worked at different organizations, does not mean that they are just as likely to work within yours— remember Taleb.

Above all, ensure that the business's leadership team understands the implications of integrating social technology into the human resources department. In the next chapter, I will be looking at how the leadership function can integrate social technology into its everyday activities too, bridging the gap between the board and employees.

CHAPTER 12

Customer Service

A socially enabled customer service team is one of the most obvious departments within a social business—with so many consumers online discussing products and services (MoneySupermarket.com and MoneySavingExpert.com have a combined 20 million unique visitors every month—and that is only the personal finance category), customer service issues are going to make up a large percentage of those conversations.

The analogy that I used recently with a client that is interested in creating a socially enabled customer service team was that with the same number of customer queries being posted online as called into the call center (if not more, honestly), ignoring the online space is the equivalent of only answering half of calls in your call center—which would be customer retention suicide. More important than this, is the fact that a phone call made to the customer care team is a purely one-to-one conversation, and if the problem cannot be resolved or they are left unsatisfied by the outcome, the customer may tell a handful of their friends later that day. A complaint online that goes unanswered or unresolved is not a one-to-one conversation, it is most certainly a one-to-many conversation that can be seen not only by the people within the complainants social graph, but by anyone searching for the terms contained within the post—as you'll remember from Chapter 7, search engines like Google prioritize social media in their search results—often positioning forums and blogs that frequently mention a business above the business's own website. That presents a potentially massive reputation issue that can only be resolved by the customer service team.

One of the most frequent complaints that I hear about customer service in general is that it is very rare for a customer service center to stay open much further outside of standard business hours, which has always dumbfounded me as most people work standard office hours, so any issues have to be resolved while the customer is at work. One of the benefits of customer complaints online is that they can be made at any time, and most customers will be forgiving if they receive a response the next day, or a few hours later. As I mentioned in an earlier chapter, the difference in how consumers prioritize their communications means that a customer complaint made over the phone is demanding on their personal time, and has to be resolved within the time frame of the call, where as a complaint made on Twitter can be responded to a number of hours later with little issue or stress, because the complaint is being made on the consumers terms, rather dictated by the hours that the business keeps. This helps to take some of the potential sting out of a customer experience that is already starting from a negative point of view.

So, how should your customer service department start to become more social in its approach to customers?

The first step is to carry out a small piece of research to gauge the volume of complaints that are currently published about your business on social platforms. The data that your research should be looking to collect should be the following:

- What is the volume of complaints made about your business online?
- How does this break down across different products and services?
- Where do the complaints take place?
- What is the sentiment breakdown of these complaints? This needs to be done manually (naturally), and scored on a *scale of negativity*, rather than a three category score (rather than positive, neutral, or negative) as the vast majority of complaints are going to be negative, but it is important to define *how negative*, in order to start to understand how to approach customer complaints in these spaces.
- What is the average reach and influence of the complaints (how many people see them, and are they regularly republished and shared)? This will help to start to understand the actual impact of customer complaints in social media, as opposed to simply looking at each complaint as a one-to-one complaint.
- How does the volume of complaints about your business fare against complaints about competitors?
- What is the average time of day the complaints are made? This will help you to plan resourcing your social customer service team.

- What does the reputation of your business look like through search?

This research project will provide you with a customer service "health check" for social media, an indication of the level of resource that will be necessary to start making an impact with social customer service issues, and a set of data with which the customer service team can benchmark itself by. Once this has been reported back into the business and resource has been budgeted for, the next step is to split complaints into two groups.

- Reactive responses to complaints that existed *prior* to the social customer service team being created (with which a decision will have to be made of which of the historic responses can still be resolved, but this is based on multiple business factors such as product lifecycle, customer lifecycle etc.).
- Proactive responses to new complaints that have been published *since* the social customer service team has been created.

As the data will already exist for the historic complaints (from the research project carried out prior to the creation of the team), the next step is to create a monitoring system for capturing new complaints—this can be as simple or complex a system as your team would like to work with, or can budget for. Initially, until the social customer service team has started to prove its business value, I would suggest using a combination of free tools that can be used manually and are easy to train employees on. Then, after the business value has been proven, the team can begin to use more complex, integrated systems such as those provided by SalesForce. com and Omniture.

RECRUITMENT AND TRAINING

The social customer service team should be recruited from internally, and experts from the customer service department should be used to ensure that the customer service that is being delivered in social spaces is of the highest quality possible—remember the one-too-many situations mentioned above, it is incredibly important to get this right, rather than moving junior or inexperienced customer service staff into a sensitive space. Overlooking the team should be a senior member from the customer service team (preferably a head of customer service) and an experienced social media or community manager that can advise on how to approach people online appropriately.

Once the team has been decided on, each member will need to go through formal social media training to ensure they are all comfortable operating in this space. This should take between half a day and a day and the following should be covered in the training session.

- A general introduction to social media and technology.
- An introduction to this specific project, outlining the objectives, strategy and implementation (channel strategy—which we will come on to later on in this chapter).
- A detailed explanation of the guidelines, the escalation process, the integration process between other departments within the business, and the approval process.
- An explanation of the regulations (if any, but we will come on to that later) that apply to the category your business is in, and the limitations that this regulation puts on the activity of the social customer service team.
- A guide to monitoring (with hands-on demonstrations of each tool that is to be used).
- A channel guide (giving hands-on demonstrations of each appropriate social platform).
- A guide to tracking and reporting.
- Case studies of successful implementations of social customer service.
- Example scenarios and best case responses.

MONITORING

The same tools that were outlined in the sales chapter (Chapter 9) can also be used within the customer service function due to the nature of how the tools operate. As previously mentioned, these tools will not guarantee that you capture *every* complaint, but at least the majority. These include (but are by no means limited to)

- TweetDeck: a simple desktop application that allows users to create multiple searches around keywords, the application then collects any tweets that use those keywords. Be careful to carefully structure your keyword searches though so as to really hone down on tweets that matter to your business.

■ Google Alerts: This service from Google will email you when certain keywords are found on new content. The service covers blog content, some forum content, and anything appearing in Google News—it is however, far from comprehensive.

■ BoardReader: This is a simple service that lets you search forums specifically using keyword strings, and then subscribe to an RSS feed of the search results, which update hourly, alerting you to any new content that is posted mentioning your keywords.

■ YouTube RSS feed for tags: YouTube lets you create an RSS feed based on certain "tags" (another word for keywords), so that when a new video is uploaded where the "tags" you selected are listed, it will update you through RSS.

(RSS feeds are "pipes" of content that you can send into an RSS feed reader, such as Google Reader. The feed reader will then display all new content on a one-page dashboard—so instead of having to visit multiple websites to check for new content, it is all sent to one place for you to read. Handy.)

REGULATION

Certain industry sectors are regulated by government bodies on what they can and cannot say to consumers, to protect consumers—sectors such as banking and pharmaceuticals being two highly regulated examples. However, this should not stop your social customer service team from responding to complaints made in social spaces, it simply means that guidelines have to be drafted, responses approved and a set of stock responses signed off by the legal and compliance departments. I have personally worked on social customer service project with both GlaxoSmithKline and MORE TH>N, both of which are heavily regulated, but providing the right preparation has been done, there really are no excuses.

CHANNELS

The research project that was carried out prior to launching the social customer service team will have indicated which platforms consumers are using to publish complaints. Your customer service channel strategy should be based on this insight, rather than choosing which network you think will be least resource intensive or the easiest to manage, as my first boss would say, "fish where the fish are."

There are, of course, a number of considerations to take into account before diving into certain channels. Below are the five most frequently used channels for consumer complaints, with the considerations to take into account.

- Twitter—the micro-blogging service has very few rules and regulations about business use, other than the threat of accounts being closed if businesses use the platform to spam users. For best practice, the O2 social customer service team does some exceptional work in the UK.
- Facebook—with over half the UK population using Facebook, it is going to be a powerful tool for the social customer service team. However, be aware that the only complaints that the team will be able to respond to will be those made on your business's Facebook page—Facebook will not allow businesses to respond to status updates, notes or anything on a user's timeline. A recommendation (based on experience) would be to consider creating a separate Facebook tab called Customer Care to try and funnel complaints away from the timeline, as this limits the visibility of the initial complaint and allows the social customer service team to deal with the issue away from the very public timeline (as well as avoiding the complaint remaining on the timeline for all fans to see.
- Forums—forums can be incredibly tricky places for businesses to navigate, and businesses that simply storm in and try and engage with the forum often find themselves in trouble with both the forum users and the moderator of the forum. If in doubt, the social customer service team needs to read all available information on businesses using the forum and contact either the moderator or the forum owner to discuss the best possible approach before starting to engage—providing that the social customer service team is using the forum to resolve problems, rather than sell products or services, the majority of the time the response is positive.
- Blogs—bloggers can be a law unto themselves, so research on each individual blogger is absolutely critical. Track back

through old blog posts, read the bloggers about page, and try and find as much information about them as possible before engaging—it may be that they react negatively to any approach by a business, or that they simply do not list contact information (in which case, try to avoid leaving a public comment on the blog unless it is absolutely necessary).

■ Review sites—each review site has different rules surrounding businesses responding to comments—some, such as TripAdvisor have come under intense scrutiny recently for being too relaxed about businesses using the platform. Review the guidelines (there are usually guidelines posted on review sites that aim to provide businesses with a list of dos and donts for posting content and responses to complaints).

ESCALATION PROCESS

The social customer service team will need to have an agreed process with the wider customer service team for escalating certain types of complaints to senior customer service staff. The best approach to this is a decision tree that provides the names of a number of different senior team members, based on the nature of the complaint.

INTERNAL INTEGRATION

Once again, one of the fundamental principles of becoming a social business is departmental integration and freely flowing information between different teams. Social customer service is likely to throw up situations where the social customer service team cannot respond because the complaint is not directly a complaint about a product, in which case it becomes a situation that the public relations department is best equipped to respond to. Agreeing on a process for this type of information sharing will lessen the burden and stress when a situation such as this arises, it will also present the customer with a smooth process that will help to stem any potentially additional frustration at being passed between different departments.

SCALABILITY AND COST SAVINGS

Scaling the social customer service team will take time, as (at least initially) the business case for investing more resource is going to have to be proven. However, once this business case has been built, the department can start to build social customer service activities into the whole department, with the team receiving calls as well as responding to complaints posted on social platforms. This is an important milestone on the journey to becoming a truly social business, but it is one that will reap serious rewards—in my experience (and unfortunately with this particular client, category sensitivities means that I cannot name the organization), successfully integrating social customer service into the whole department can have the following impact on the business;

- Improve customer satisfaction scores.
- Increase customer retention/loyalty.
- Increase brand consideration.
- Increase positive word of mouth and awareness (positively resolved customers *will* share their experience on social platforms).
- Vastly improve business reputation on search engine results pages.
- Increase the number of customers that each member of the customer service team can respond to (with the unnamed client, introducing social customer service meant that the customer service team could deal with and resolve five complaints for every one customer care call that came through on the phones— this lead to a massive reduction in customer service costs).

The last point usually has the most resonance with the leadership function, as customer service departments and call centers can cost tens of millions of pounds a year to maintain, so any significant reduction in costs that can be achieved is going to have a profound impact on reducing business overheads.

AMPLIFICATION OF RESOLUTIONS

Once the social customer service team has become comfortable working in this space, you can start to work with other departments in the business to promote complaints that have been resolved and the testimonials that have been received from satisfied customers— this data can be used across various marketing and advertising media, including; direct mail, the website, paid media, creative,

PPC (SEO), and media relations. Successfully resolved customer care situations often help convert the customer from a negative detractor of the business, to a high-praising ambassador—which is especially powerful in social spaces.

SOCIAL CUSTOMER RELATIONSHIP MANAGEMENT

I believe that one of the most exciting aspects of launching a social customer service team is the ability to use the social data that is gathered to include in existing customer relationship management (CRM) systems—this is where integration can really prove its worth. Tracking complaints is a standard activity within customer service departments, it has to be, but adding additional customer social data to this system can have a number of benefits that can then have a positive impact on numerous departments across the whole business. The perfect social CRM system would track the following types of social data:

- Social profiles (does the customer use Twitter, Facebook, do they have a blog, are they active on forums?)
- Social footprint (how influential is the customer, what is their audience reach, how frequently do they publish content?)

This information could then be shared with the following departments:

- Data
  - ☐ What insights can we derive from this customer's social information?
- Marketing and advertising
  - ☐ How can we use the information gathered from the customer's social information to improve our strategic proposition?
- Public relations
  - ☐ Does the customer have considerable influence? Can we add them to our influencer database?
- Research and development
  - ☐ Would the customer be interested in helping us to develop new products and improve existing propositions?

- Human resources
  - ☐ Does the customer have any existing connections to an employee of the business?

Let us briefly look at a scenario:

- A customer publishes a complaint about the business on Twitter.
- The social customer service team responds to the complaint, resolving the issue within an hour.
- The complaint, resolution and social profile data is then logged by the social customer service team.
- This data is then fed through to the social CRM database manager, who updates the customer's records.
- A few days later, the customer receives an email from the direct marketing team asking how their experience was with the social customer service team—providing a unique link to the business's Facebook page where the customer is invited to take part in proposition testing with the research and development team because the business values their feedback.

This is incredibly powerful integration that relies heavily on the smooth transition of data across the organization, but once those processes and systems have been set up, the effect should be immediately noticeable as the business begins to present a single brand image, rather than four, five or six slightly different brand images.

CHAPTER 13

Leadership (Redux)

After the previous six chapters, I think it is important to quickly revisit the ten tenets of social business, before we conclude on this book and we all move on to create stronger businesses (I hope).

Always remember:

- **Focus on data**
- Feed your organization with social data from customers—the data *is* your market.
- Data is not just external, use data to better understand your workforce.
- Keep the data flowing, that way your organization is always on, always learning.

- **Focus on being reactive**
- Listen to your market, learn how it moves and who influences it and then react to the changes.
- Customer feedback does not always need to be implemented, but it should always be listened to.
- Cut down research and development time by using social data and testing, and create lean teams that are prepared to launch beta products.

- **Focus on people**
- Your business is your people, whether they are your employees or your market. Give them your attention.
- Create the right culture and your business will feel like a movement—both employees and the market will defend you and protect you.
- Understand networks of people, how messages and information move within them, how they change and how you can be part of them.

- **Focus on retention**
- If your business can keep its customers happy, they will become more embedded. They will tell your brand story, they will tell their friends about your products and services.
- Not only is it cheaper to keep staff happy, but they will also build a much stronger bond with your business—having a revolving door will damage your SBTs.
- The best acquisition strategy is a good retention strategy—cut churn, improve satisfaction, and boost profitability.

- **Focus on being open**
- An open business is not some Silicon Valley idealistic, bean-bags-in-reception type approach, it is allowing skills, expertise, and data to flow (unrestricted) through your business. The best people, and the best data, for the job.
- Allow your market, your influencers and your critics into your business—they can only make it better. Open business is about transparency and honesty.
- Stop pushing your "brand" and focus on delivering your "business"—a brand voice can sound disingenuous and corporate, giving your employees a voice will let the market see the humans inside your business.

- **Focus on culture**
- Culture cannot be created, it must be guided and it can only come from your employees—having training days paintballing is a sticking plaster on your organization's culture, fix the fundamentals.
- Your culture needs to reflect your ambition to be a social business—let people talk to each other, learn from each other and enjoy what they do.
- If you follow these tenets, you are more likely to create a culture of pride—when people work to create products and services that make people's lives better, they feel proud of what they do.

- **Focus on innovation**
- Your business is only as good as its last product and every time you get ahead of the game, another business is going to be working harder to beat you—never stop innovating.

- The opportunity for innovation can come from anywhere or anyone, but it has to be granted to employees through culture and trust. Trust your employees.
- If your organization gets complacent and stops listening to the market, you will lose market share, you will lose your best employees, and ultimately, you will fail.

Focus on integration
- If your business is going to be open and innovative, that is going to involve breaking down your organization's silos.
- Integration is not just about internal communications, it is also about integrating with your market. Find your business's role in the market.
- Great ideas are not the preserve of the creative—creativity is everywhere, you just need to promote integration to unlock it.

Focus on your business
- If your products and services are not delivering the right value to your market, no one will care about your brand.
- A two-page spread in the Wall Street journal on your business is great, but never forget who pays the bills.
- Focus on fixing your business first, do not rely on a great "brand image" to paper over the cracks. Social technology is like make-up remover.

Focus on the meaningful
- So few businesses give a true focus to the meaningful—learn what makes a difference to your business, and improve it.
- Avoid vanity. At all costs.
- Your business needs to create meaning for employees and the market—that can only come from understanding what those two groups find is meaningful.

CHAPTER 14

Conclusion

Hopefully by this point you have come to your own conclusions, but there is a good chance that the last 60,000 words could have fallen into a ramble or rant, so if you have not, I will summarize my thoughts now.

THE REVOLUTIONS CONTINUE

Over the last few hundred years there have been numerous revolutions; industrial, cultural, technological; and all of them have brought us to where we stand today; at the start of the next revolution. This decade started by the dot-com bubble, driven by enthusiasm for the brave new world, investors rushed to cash in, unaware that many of the platforms being built were made of straw. With the recent IPO from Facebook, many people are predicted a second bubble (at the time of writing, and the time of print, it will be far too early to predict whether this is happening—if Taleb teaches us anything, it is not to micro-analyze small shifts in share price), but from the perspective of business leaders, what we need to be looking at is not how much media attention social networks and media get, but instead how we can look at those technologies and use them to improve our business—and not just our marketing department.

Too many people believe that social media is about technology, it is not; it is about people and the access that the technology gives us to communicate with those people. I reiterate, social media is not about technology, it is about people. I have been witness to far too many presentations where an agency has created a beautifully presented strategy that fails to comprehend this—you do not need a Facebook, Twitter or blogger strategy, you need to understand how people want to interact with your business, not your brand, your business.

NO ONE CARES ABOUT YOUR BRAND

I am sure this will rile up the brand managers reading this, and it is a terribly didactic comment to make, but *no one cares about your brand*. It used to be that the "brand" provided the salience on the shelf, the differentiation between two almost identical products, but people have become more demanding and have greater access to information like reviews, advice and peer-support. If your product or service does not deliver, the brand will not save it. If your product or service does deliver, your brand can enhance it, and people will want to hear more about your brand story—it is at this point that storytelling becomes important, because people are going to be much more receptive to it than if they have had a negative experience with your business in the past.

I believe that this shift comes from two sources: the economy and technology.

With a weak economy (understatement of the decade) comes increased pressure on consumer spending—people are less likely to take risks and more likely to either stick to what they know works, or purchase things that are virtually guaranteed to be what they need. This type of spending is harmful to businesses looking to launch new products without testing them in an agile way first—but it could be massively beneficial for businesses that listen to people, and produce products and services that they are currently asking, if not begging, for in conversations taking place right now. If a business can start to listen to this raw data, and process it properly, that business will set to make a lot of people very happy, and the shareholders ecstatic.

Technology has played an incredibly important role for two reasons: (1) it is now easier for people to find out information about your products and services from other people that have used them, and (2) once someone has used your product or service, they have an immediate network with which to share their experience with—creating a virtuous circle of sharing. It does not have to be a negative story businesses though; they can contribute to these conversations that take place (providing the business approaches them in the right way) and resolve issues, offer advice, share knowledge and loosen up a little! Constantly churning out corporate speak, and being defensive and secretive is a sure fire way to have people react in a negative way against your business—just reread *The Cluetrain*

Manifesto (I will presume (and hope) that you have already read it at least once).

When you tie these two factors together (fear of risk and access to peer-review), you have the perfect storm for consumers becoming less deferent to products and services. It is late 2012 and the Euro-crisis is in full swing—there is a strong chance that the economy is not going to returning to joyful boom times for at least a few years and businesses need to understand that these two factors are going to be the difference between an increase in profitability and increasing retention of customers and employees and having to close up shop, leaving empty offices all over the world.

EMBRACE COMPLEXITY IN YOUR ORGANIZATION

One of the important cultural challenges in business that opposes this is the tendency to lean toward simplicity, rather than complexity, and nowhere else is this more evident than in demographic research. As previously explored, the concept of "demographics" as a means of mass marketing to certain segments of consumers has been shattered by the increasingly visible splintering of the very same consumer groups—with many businesses now spending tens of millions every year to try and isolate who their key demographic is; is it the Capitalist Eco-Warrior profile? Or could it be the Dulwich Mum 2.0? This continuing disintegration of market segments is only going to continue as trends and lifestyles become much more fractured—again, due in part to technology, but that is a whole different book altogether.

So how can your business shed the market demographic baggage? Well, as discussed in Chapter 9, finding new customers is as straightforward as understanding their behavior, which can be done through finding the communities that they talk in. Then it is just a case of identifying who is actively looking to make a purchase and starting to build a relationship with them. In terms of cost and scale, this is done by the sales force, and as with customer service, the volume of sales that you can make online far outweighs the volume of sales you can make either in person or even on the phone. So your sales force is making more sales, in less time and you are saving vast amounts of money on detailed market research *and* better than that, you are talking directly to your consumers— the best market research there is, because they *are* your market.

Speaking to consumers can obviously be a challenge, and as outlined earlier in the book, giving your employees a voice helps, as does defining your businesses voice online. However, businesses cannot escape from the idea of *business intention* versus *consumer reception*. Once a piece of content or an idea is out on social media, it becomes part of the community itself, and the reception it receives can have multiple outcomes—this exemplifies why it is absolutely critical to ensure that the voice of your business and your employees is human. Even the most human of brands (think Innocent, or Ford) still encounter crossed wires and misinterpretation from time to time, but preparation is key and as long as you stick to simple principles, your ambassadors and advocates will defend you so that you do not have to defend yourself.

DIGITAL NATIVES ARE YOUR FUTURE MARKET

Of course all of this is going to be made much more simple as the next generation of business leaders rise through the ranks, with little experience of life without an Internet connection—their entire existence to date has been converged, so they are going to expect the same of their workplace. Their ideas will be integrated, their business thinking the same, and this is going to (over time) change the face of business. However, this is not an excuse to sit back and wait for someone else to do all the work, because as well as the future of your workforce existing in this converged world, your future market is going to be in the same world too—and they are going to expect change much faster. Mobile, digital, experiential, CRM, recruitment, media relations—the next generation of consumers are not going to see your brand in a traditional sense, they are going to expect it to be fully integrated. If they call to purchase a new product, they are going to expect to be asked whether they would like to be contacted by email, phone or mail in the future, but also Twitter, or Facebook or instant messenger. You only have to look at the mountain of research that points toward text and IM addiction in people under 16 to see that communication is based on convenience, and a phone call, as my old boss Stuart Bruce used to say, is highly demanding on your time. It requires immediate action, whereas an instant message or a tweet allows you to respond in your own time—you might not agree with this approach, but the research is mounting up and these are your businesses future consumers.

BREAKING DOWN THE CORPORATE WALLS

When you combine this with rising consumer expectations of brands, it becomes evident that breaking down the walls of your business and becoming more involving with both consumers and employees is an important stepping stone to becoming a social business. With trust in businesses falling year on year (see the previously referenced Edelman Trust Barometer research from 2012), businesses are going to have to combat this by being more open, more transparent, and giving the people within the walls a voice of their own that is free of stringent guidelines and restrictions, and devoid of any corporate buzzwords. People currently trust people like themselves, so if you pressure employees into talking like a press release, you are going to damage the potential strength of relationship that they can have with your market. Like the Sun Tzu parable in *The Art of War* explains, if your business is built like a castle upon a hill, the villagers are going to revolt, but if you live with the villagers your business will be the business of the people. Break down the invisible corporate walls, invite your customers in and let your employees build relationships with the market.

By opening the door to your business, you are opening the door to raw consumer insights—I used to work with SilverCross, a wonderful pushchair brand steeped in heritage, and my first project with them was speaking directly to parents on popular parenting forums NetMums and MumsNet. What started as an initial chat about its product range became an ongoing conversation, resulting in some of the forum members being invited into the factory to see where improvements could be made—this type of open approach is powerful for two reasons: (1) you are involving your market in product development, and (2) they are going to talk about this experience with their social networks. Primarily though, this is about involving your market, the secondary benefit is that "word of mouth" kicks in and all of a sudden people begin to talk about your business as a social business—but you have to prove this first, there are not vanity projects in an open, transparent business, because trying to fake your way through innovation can have devastating consequences and cause huge backlash online—for evidence of this, just look at Wal-Mart's Wal-Marting across America campaign that was launched in 2006 that featured two seemingly nonpartisan everyday people who had decided to take a camper van across America visiting (and blogging about) their experiences with different Wal-Mart stores—it was eventually uncovered that the two people were employed by Edelman, Wal-Mart's public relations agency, and the first "social media" crisis was created—with a riotous response from people online who felt that they had been taken in and made fools of by the campaign.

So transparency in your business is important, not only to avoid negative reactions and backlash, but to build trust with your market. If people within your organization can build trust with the market, the relationship can be fruitful for both parties and the business can speak regularly to the market and ask questions. As mentioned in Chapter 10, Unilever is doing just that with its Unilever VIP program through Facebook. Mutual trust is an incredibly powerful tool for a business and a community to possess, and it can help to build better products and services; better products, improved retention and, ultimately, smarter, more social businesses with better profitability.

DATA-DRIVEN, HUMAN BUSINESS

There is a dichotomy that I am sure you have figured out already, but what I have suggested over the last few chapters is that you need to become a more human business, by using technology and data more efficiently (or using it all). I appreciate this is a little paradoxical, however, remember that you are using raw human data to improve your business and *become* more human as a business. The data will be the foundation that your business is built on, but it will allow you to open your doors and invite people in, to create a human tone of voice while giving your employees their own voice, helping you to create products and services that people, humans, want. Without the data, just the human voice, your business will struggle to scale, with just the data and none of the voice, you will become a faceless (and, frankly) terrifying business that cannot communicate with either employees or consumers, but the right balance of the two will see your business soar. Just remember one thing; your business is making products and delivering services that people want, and your staff are delivering this as humans—it is the perfect combination to become a market leader.

A SOCIAL BUSINESS IS NOT BUILT OVERNIGHT

This notion of "social business" is currently very en vogue, but most who pontificate about it are still looking at business as if it were just a marketing function. The fundamental aspect that most "social media ninjas" miss is that marketing provides a tiny fraction of the business benefit that being more social can bring your organization. Social business is about understanding your consumers with the greatest depth possible—inviting them in to be part of the fabric of your business. There is only one way to achieve this though, and it has to come from the senior leadership function—this is cultural and technological change at it is most grandiose, but also at it is most potentially fruitful. Everyone wants to work somewhere where people understand and value them, to produce products that people enjoy and to be part of something. It is in our biological nature to want to be part of something successful, and that can only be lead by those at the top table. Over the next five years, you are going to have visits from countless management consultants and "evangelists" that are trying to sell two-day workshops on how to become a "truly social business," but trust me, embedding social technology into your business's DNA and understanding how to use that level of raw human insight is a cultural and technological shift that cannot be covered by a two-day workshop from someone who once read a copy of *Fast Company* and has a Twitter account with 5000 followers.

It is also important for me to explain one of the potential negative aspects of becoming a social business—there is no turning back. Once you have started to build relationships with consumers and employees, you cannot change your mind. Just remember the old adage, *Go Big or Go Home*, because that is never been as relevant as it is with social business. Once you have started to deliver the service that people are craving, and produce products that people adore, you are going to have to keep that up. And the expectation will grow, not because consumers will pressure you, but because they are going to tell their friends about this amazing company they have found, and then their friends will become part of the fabric too, then they will tell their friends, and on and on, until your business is the market leader, which brings with it a lot of pressure, but also a lot of happy employees and customers, and there are certainly worse situations to be in.

The day that you start to make changes, there is going to be reactions—both positive and negative. Not everyone is comfortable being part of an "open business," but they will, as time goes on and they see the benefits that it brings, people will embrace the new way. Having an open business is about flattening out hierarchies and tearing away bureaucratic corporate culture—you do not have to become a business with a slide from the top floor to the reception, or beanbags in meeting rooms, but you do have to become a business where everyone enjoys their job and feels part of something, part of something special, because if you can make ambassadors of your employees, when they inevitably talk about where they work, be it in a bar or on Facebook, they are going to do so with pride. And they will defend you.

ACCOUNTABLE AND INNOVATIVE BUSINESS

Change is hard, but open business also means accountable business, whether that is understanding which ideas have or have not worked or understanding which employee has or has not delivered. By breaking down departmental silos we will quickly see who makes a massive difference to the business. My first industry mentor, Tim Sinclair, the chairman of Wolfstar, told me on my first day that all that matters when it comes to employees is "do you make a difference to my business?" and if you do, you will always be safe, and that has stuck with me for the last six years—it is a great mantra to have because it forces you to strive to always have impact. Once your business becomes open, and data can be tracked across every department, it will become evident who makes a difference.

Through this level of fluidity throughout business, and the rise of the Chief Data Officer, your business should also see an increase in its ability to be reactive and agile—moving on new information faster than ever before and being able to turn around new products and services within record time—after all, your staff are now hyper-networked and knowledge sharing is companywide, so every employee knows the best person for the job. As you can see, this becomes incredibly powerful, and the organization starts to live and breathe like an organism—my favorite analogy is of the centipede and the ants; if you create a business culture of ants, everyone runs off to do their own thing, playing their own individual part but never sure of the end goal, whereas if you create a business like a centipede then each leg moves toward one common end goal. Build a centipede.

BECOMING EVERYTHING, TO EVERYONE

For the last two or three years digital and media commentators have been predicting the rise of "the social business"—and there are a few starting to crop up, but most are born from digital ideas that then move offline—businesses like Spotify—so social technology is already built into their DNA. However, the real challenge is going to be making the cultural and technological shift inside an existing, traditional business, but it is going to happen, because the market is demanding it. What this will look like in five years time is a difficult prediction to make (and again, theories of economic fragility from both Mandelbrot and Taleb teach us not to make predictions) but hopefully we will have much more innovative markets as different businesses develop multiple differentiated products that serve more niche, but multiple audiences, rather than single products aimed at the masses. The level of innovation that social data provides will allow for this, and by working with consumers, businesses will acquire more customers than they could ever imagine—building products and services that people want, and retaining those customers *because* the business has become social. The managing director at VCCP Share (my current agency), Dominic Stinton, has spent the last 20 years working on some of the world's most famous (and successful) advertising campaigns and there is barely a week that goes by without him telling me that "your brand should mean something different to everyone, but it should always have a voice, a point of view and a foundation"— your brand can have variations on its products without diluting the brand—just look at Nike and its cultural, sports and leisure brand footprint. Every brand impression is different, and this is what makes Nike a global super brand.

This is the level of innovation that the market is coming to expect, and hopefully over the last few chapters I have helped explain my vision of how businesses can achieve that.

Without wanting to turn the final chapter into a manifesto for change (although now I have said it, it inadvertently is just that), I believe that there are five guiding principles to becoming a social business. These five points are the essence of everything that I have written about in the previous chapters, and if you decide to recommend this book to anyone, then perhaps save them some time by pointing to this page. My five guiding principles are as follows:

1. **Remember what hits the bottom line, a "Like" is meaningless without a purchase**
    The purpose of the last 60,000 words is to help integrate social technology across your business, to give you greater access to the most important asset you have—people. It is important to remember, though, that conversations on their own are meaningless unless there is action—just like Elvis said. If you set clear objectives that are aligned to your business goals (whatever they may be) and work carefully to create an actionable and pragmatic strategy, then you will hit those business objectives. This goes for any department, and while marketing is currently *le enfant terriblé* when it comes to vanity metrics, it will not be long before every other department is playing the same game. Work toward integrating social technology into your business and avoid adding "something a bit social media" onto existing work. This will help to create a clear and accountable return on investment, and hopefully (in my experience) help your business to reduce costs, increase revenue and produce more innovative and in-demand products and services.

2. **The world is converging, your business must do the same**
    The next generation of consumers cannot remember a time without a mobile phone or access to the Internet. Their lives are lived not online and offline, but integrated—the two worlds have converged and if your business is to keep the "open" sign on the door, your business has to reflect this new world. This point remains for both consumers *and* employees—the important thing is that your ageing leadership function needs to understand (not necessarily live in, but understand) this new world and all the benefits that it is going to bring to the bottom line. The business arrogance of the 1960s and the rule of tyrannical brands are over. The walls of your business are falling at an exponential rate (weirdly similar to Moore's Law, eh?) and now is the time to act to ensure that your employees and consumers feel like they are a part of your business—because it is time to involve them. Let the walls fall.

3. **Always listen to the network, but you do not have to always react**
    Understanding both your internal and external network has
    never been so important, from influential pockets of employees,
    and analysts sharing corporate secrets on ZeroHedge, to media
    requests through Twitter and grassroots protests about your
    latest recipe for your most popular product—understanding
    these networks is probably the most important factor in becom-
    ing a social business. Understand the network, the dynamics,
    the data and the information flow and the rest should follow.
    However, understanding and responding to are *not* the same.
    If a business responded to every single status update and user-
    generated video, there would never be any time to produce
    products or deliver service—context is king, and always take
    into account the wider space. A handful of complaints about
    a product that sells millions of units every day deserve to be
    listened to, but changing the aspect that people are complain-
    ing about runs the risk of upsetting the millions of consumers
    while only appeasing a handful.
4. **Do not shy away from complexity, instead, lean toward it**
    This is probably the hardest principle to stomach, as it stands
    against centuries of businesses trying to simplify everything
    from market research to factory production, except we have
    little choice but to embrace the chaos. In times of technological,
    societal and economic fragility, your business needs to present
    the face of simplicity, yet underneath be dealing with the com-
    plexity. Dealing with it is not easy, but through embracing cha-
    otic networks, Big Data and open business you will find that
    your business becomes much more simple, just by embracing
    the complexity within.
5. **Data is the new oil, you just need to know where to find it to
    get rich**
    The currency of social technology is data—access to it, the
    opportunity to interact with it, and (most importantly) the
    opportunity to use it to build better products. This currency is
    easily translatable into market, competitor and human insights,
    beating focus groups hands down. Your market research just
    went from a sample of 1000 people across five socioeconomic
    demographics to 4 billion people, across 4 billion different
    socioeconomic demographics. Use it wisely though, because
    every single one of those people might be watching.

The future of business is social, whether we like it or not, and the leaders of tomorrow's global businesses have to embrace this, not because marketing or management consultants instruct them to, but because their markets are instructing them to. Everything I have laid out over the last 14 chapters has been proven with global businesses. So, if you try it with your business and it does not work, give me a call. Until then, all the best.

The future is now, your business just does not know it yet, but it will do soon.

Notes

Introduction

1. Nassim Nicholas Taleb, *The Bed of Procrustes*, p. 56. Allen Lane, London, 2010 (England).

1 The Death of "Brand"

1. http://the-logic-group.net/pv_obj_cache/pv_obj_id_ F527A2314D0913015CC2D21AB16550444CFC3300/filename/ The%20Imperatives%20for%20Customer%20Loyalty%20 2011.pdf, January 2012.
2. Google Trends, February 2012.
3. GroupM Search Whitepaper, 2011.

3 Embracing Complexity

1. Changing Places, Spencer Stuart, 2011—http://www.spencerstuart. com/articleview-zmags.aspx?id=91bb89f9
2. http://www.youtube.com/watch?v=jlId_iOLmjk
3. http://www.pps.org/reference/hans-monderman/
4. http://www.nytimes.com/2011/08/14/opinion/sunday/the-elusive-big-idea.html?_r=4&pagewanted=all
5. http://techcrunch.com/2010/08/04/schmidt-data/

4 The Role of Data

1. http://www.zephoria.org/thoughts/archives/2010/04/17/ big-data-opportunities-for-computational-and-social-sciences. html
2. http://www.economist.com/node/15557443?story_id=15557443
3. http://www.statowl.com/search_engine_market_share.php

5 An Introduction to Social Business

1. *The Social Media MBA*, Wiley, London (2011).

10 Research and Development

1. Nicholas Taleb, *The Bed of Procrustes*, p. 60.

Index